A Guide to

Immigration Law of the **United States of America**

ISBN: 978-1-7350407-0-7 Paperback

INTRODUCTION

Welcome!

My aim with this book is to try and simplify immigration law a bit so that the layman can understand it.

Of course, it is impossible to cover every aspect and every nuance of the law in one short document. I did not try to do this but tried rather to give an overview that could help you if you want to come to America.

It can also be that you are already here and want to change your residency status. This book can help you.

I know I would have found it helpful to have a resource such as this book when I first came to America. Unfortunately, nothing like this was available. Luckily, I was helped by a few generous people.

This book is my way of 'paying it forward.' I hope that I can, in some small way, help you make a positive change in your life.

Sincerely yours

Levan Natalishvili

Natalishvili Law Firm, PLLC
225 Broadway, Suite 630
New York, New York 10007
Tel: (212) 791-7500

CONTENTS

A Guide to
Immigration Law of the United States of America

Levan Natalishvili

CHAPTER 1

You are holding this book because you want to know more about immigrating to the United States.

You are not alone! Thousands of people – also from Georgia and Russia – immigrate to the US every year. Before 1970, most immigrants to the US came from Mexico. Since 2009, the makeup of newcomers changed. Countries like India, China, the Dominican Republic, the Philippines, and Cuba have seen sizable immigration to the US.

I have written this booklet because I believe I am in a unique position to help you. Today, I am an immigration lawyer, but once I was also in your shoes.

My story

I am from Georgia. As you'd probably know, the 1990s was a turbulent time in our country. The post-Soviet transitional era was problem-ridden and unsafe.

I was lucky. I got accepted into a United States college in Nashville, Tennessee. My brother was already in the US, living in New York at that time. I took the opportunity to come to America. However, I had no intention of staying permanently.

I completed my first semester in Nashville but fell in love with New York and all its diversity during visits to my brother. I changed to Hunter College and continued my studies there. I studied hard and worked hard. I took sporadic odd jobs – from part-time to full-time to make ends meet.

It was not easy for me to adapt to living in the United States. As any immigrant would attest, the challenges are numerous. I was lucky to have my brother, but we had to deal with a lot of trials, jointly and independently.

Nashville was culturally a world apart from Georgia. I stuck out like a sore thumb. In New York, I felt more at home because of the city's diversity.

In retrospect, I would perhaps do some things differently. What helped though, is that I met people who were professional and able to give me sound advice.

It is something that I cannot stress enough: you need to create a network for yourself when you come to the US. Everyone needs someone professional to bounce ideas off – whether it is about matters in general or legalities. Friends and family cannot always provide all the correct answers.

Your reason for coming to the US

Like me, thousands of people decide to move to the US every year. The reasons are many and varied.

Perhaps you want to study (like I did) or you want that dream job. You may want to come and retire in the US or invest in the country. Perhaps you have family here.

If you are persecuted in your country because of your political or religious views, you might also decide that immigration is an option for you. You might be fleeing from an abusive relationship.

Some people only want to come on a temporary basis to work or study. There is an opportunity for them too, utilizing different visa options from the US government.

You might crave a better education that is not possible in your country. It is possible to come and study in the US on an F-1 visa just like I did.

A temporary visa may turn into a permanent one, because circumstances change. A US green card may be in your future.

Whatever your reason for immigration, the United States is a country of economic diversity. It is a vast country and offers jobs in almost every industry.

You need a valid visa

The very first thing you need to do when you are considering immigrating to the US is to understand that you do need a valid visa to enter and to live in the US legally.

There are several categories of visas you can apply for. My aim here is to explain some options for certain visas to you so that you can make an informed decision.

There are four main pathways to a green card: through employment sponsorship (this includes all the EB classifications – EB-1-5 – which can lead to a green card), through family, as a refugee or as a winner of the DV lottery. There are also certain visas that allow individuals to study or work in the USA.

The whole process can be very stressful. Not only do you have to apply for a visa, but most likely, you also must find work in the US and relocate your family.

I understand. I've lived it myself. I came to the US at first under an F-1 student visa. I was able to stay permanently after I won a DV lottery visa.

I, too, had to have professional help to get my green card to permanent residency.

Work as a non-immigrant

It is also possible to work in the US as a non-immigrant.

<u>But it is important to note</u> that you will need a specific visa, based on the type of work you will be doing. No-one can legally work in the US without authorization. Tourists are not allowed to work at all.

Many people choose this route first to get their foot in the door. They apply for an O-1 visa, the P-level visa or an E-2 visa. However, these types of visas do not guarantee you a green card, although they can help in obtaining one.

Let us help

We will show you what to do – step by step. There are multiple options to work and live in the US legally. I believe that each person and his/her situation is unique. I will help you get to the US in a way that fits your personality and lifestyle.

I can help you:

- Save time.
- Fill out all the necessary paperwork.
- Sift through all the visa options and find one that fits your situation.

Your social-work lawyer

Before I became a lawyer, I was a social worker. I am, therefore, in the best position to advise you about issues that immigrants face once they land in the US.

My clients report that they find the language barrier and cultural differences daunting. Some struggle with prejudice and isolation, whether real or perceived. They worry about their kids.

How to find work and housing? It can be stressful. Once you are settled in, you'd want to get access to services and transportation. It can be challenging to understand how everything works.

When I first came to the US, I had no clue what a credit score was! I wanted to rent an apartment, but landlords requested rigorous financial documentation from me that I did not understand. It was tough for me to be able to rent my first apartment.

Today, immigrants and students still find this hard, though it might be a bit easier nowadays with the evolution of social media and smartphones.

I am not saying it will be easy once you get to the United States. But at least you'd have someone at your side who knows what it is like. I've lived it.

Today, I would like to think I am a successful immigration lawyer. And mainly because I am in a position to provide real help to people that impacts their very lives.

How did I get here?

I studied hard and earned my bachelor's degree in Psychology in 1999. I got a job as a social worker at the Jewish Association Serving the Aging (JASA). I had to assist senior citizens with a variety of issues.

I also worked as a domestic violence counselor at the New York

Association for New Americans (NYANA). This was the preeminent organization in New York that helped millions of immigrants to immigrate and resettle in the USA.

I decided to pursue my master's degree in Psychology.

After graduation in 2003, I worked at the Young Adult Institute (YAI), which helps people with developmental disabilities. Today, YAI is still one of the leading organizations with innovative ideas on how to assist people with disabilities so they can utilize their full potential for a more enriching life.

After working in the field for ten years, I discovered that I liked helping people and that I wanted to have some legal background to do it most effectively.

So, I went to school. I graduated law school in 2008, passed the bar in 2009, and in 2010 after briefly working for a law firm, opened my own practice. I have been practicing since.

I am passionate about helping people. I would also like to help you.

◆ ◆ ◆

CHAPTER 2

IS IT POSSIBLE FOR ME TO MOVE TO THE US?

You might be wondering if you can move to the US. Yes, you know thousands have done it before you, but the process looks so intimidating. You are wondering if you will be able to do it.

In this chapter, I would like to share a bit of my personal story to encourage you.

It **is** possible to immigrate, leave your home country, and start a new, prosperous life in the US. But I won't sugarcoat it – the decision is not easy, and there are lots of aspects to consider. Your expectations must be realistic.

As I told you in the previous chapter, I came to the United States as a student under an F-1 visa. My loving parents and brother were very supportive.

(I have had many clients since who came to America on a tourist visa and decided to stay to pursue education. It is possible to change your status to F-1 once in the US, although it is becoming increasingly difficult. One must plan it carefully.)

I had no choice where to go. My college destination was chosen for me. Those years, we did not have much support or information from the US. Today, it is better, with information to be found on the Internet and from professionals like myself.

I thought America would be like in the movies!

I was surprised by the traditional and quiet Nashville. Everything was different – from the culture to the academic life and the legalities of staying.

The advice I give someone today who is considering coming to the US to work and live?

First, you must know why you want to come. Secondly, how to do it? A strategy is important.

An F-1 student, for instance, is only allowed to study in the US. It is a non-immigration visa. However, there are limited circumstances where you might be permitted to work while studying. Depending on the education you received and the degree you get, you might even be able to work for a limited time in the US after graduation.

If you would like to stay on (like I did), you must explore other options that can lead to your green card. But, if your plan is only to get a US-based education and then return to your country, the F-1 would be the best strategy for you.

How can I help in your immigration matters?

- I know what it is like. I came to the US myself as a student in 1994.

- I've worked with the immigrant population for more than a decade as a social worker and nearly ten years as a lawyer. I can empathize with you. I know your struggles.

- I've helped many, many people immigrate to the United States successfully.

◆ ◆ ◆

CHAPTER 3
TEMPORARY MID- TO MEDIUM-TERM VISAS

There are two ways of going about legally working in the US

Work temporarily as a non-immigrant

As a first option, you can work temporarily, as a non-immigrant. As discussed above, it might be your strategy to gain work experience or see what it is like to live in a foreign country for a while. All along, your intention might be to return to your home country eventually.

Under US immigration law, your prospective employer must file a petition to be able to hire you. US Citizenship and Immigration Services (USCIS) must approve the request before you can apply for a work visa. Any visa application with an H, L, O, P or Q in its name must go through this process.

Approval of a petition does not necessarily mean that a visa will be allocated to you. You can still be disqualified under US immigration laws while going through the process.

Work and live permanently as an immigrant

The second way to gain access to the US is to apply for a green card. If you follow this route, and if you are successful, you will gain permanent residency to the US.

In this chapter, we will look at a few different options available to you in these two categories.

Please keep in mind that there are loads of different visa options. For a complete list, please visit the website of U.S. Citizenship and Immigration Services.

The purpose of this booklet is to illustrate some of the most common ways that people have utilized my services and how I was able to help them.

Temporary mid- to medium-term visas

1. The F-1 Visa for students

What is an F-1 visa?

The F-1 visa is a non-immigrant visa. It allows foreign nationals to study in the United States. You can attend a language training program, a seminary, a high school, college, university, or any other academic institution under the F-1 visa.

What about my family?

F-1 visa holder dependents are also allowed to come to the US – on an F-2 visa.

The F-2 visa, however, is extremely limited. Children can go to school, but a spouse on the F-2 is not allowed to work.

Technically, it would be possible to change your status to an H-1B visa, but it is not easy. A US employer must be willing to sponsor you and your job needs to be a specialty occupation. (See our information on the H-1B visa later in this booklet.) A spouse on an F-2 visa may have other options. Speak to me so that we can determine the best strategy for you.

The F-1 visa process

The process discussed here is what to do if applying for the F-1 visa outside of the US.

- The first step in the process is to apply to a US school that has been approved by the Student and Exchange Visitor Program (SEVP.)

- There are many great academic institutions across America, but not all are equipped to handle international students. There is an administrative process that may be daunting to some schools. So, before you fill in application forms or write essays, it is essential to verify that the school you would like to attend is on the SEVP list.

- Once a school or an academic institution accepts you, you'll be officially enrolled into the SEVP. A one-time application fee must be paid.

- Once this is in place, you'll be given an I-20 form. This form will allow you to schedule your appointment with your local US consulate where someone will interview you.

- The purpose of the interview is to determine if you are qualified to receive an F-1 student visa. You should take along all your relevant documents and be prepared to answer personal questions about why you want to study in the US.

- If approved, you must pay a visa fee. Your fingerprints will be taken digitally and you must hand in your passport for visa issuance.

Will I qualify for an F-1 visa?

To qualify for an F-1 visa, a potential student would need to prove:

- Official residence in his/her country.

- That he/she intends to return home. The intention of the F-1 visa is for further education and taking your new-found knowledge home. The idea is not for you to remain in the US. If an interviewer gets an inkling of that, it is most likely that your visa will be denied.

- Going together with the previous requirement, another part of your F-1 interview would be to prove to the officer that you have strong ties to your home country. You must be able to show that your family are important to you, that you have bank accounts in your home country, as well as other assets. If you can prove that you have a firm job offer upon your return after getting your qualification, it would be great!

- You must show that you've been accepted by an SEVP-approved institution.

- Your opportunities to legally work in the US will be extremely limited under the F-1 visa. Therefore, you must be able to show that your living and study expenses will be covered for as long as you are in the US. It is not cheap to study in the US. A solid financial plan showing how you are going to do it is therefore crucial to pass your F-1 visa interview.

Working on my F-1 visa

Remember, the F-1 visa is intended for full-time students.

International students can work however, on campus, while school is in session. The limit on this is 20 hours per week. During holidays, students can work full-time, but only with approval from the Department of Homeland Security (DHS) and the international office of your sponsoring school.

It is a serious offence to work illegally on an F-1 visa, and you could be placed in removal proceedings if found out.

An exception to the rule is Optional Practical Training (OPT) that allows F-1 students to train (and therefore in essence, to work) off-campus in an area related to their field of study. You must ask permission to be able to do this.

Things are not working out. Can I transfer schools on my F-1 visa?

It is possible to transfer to another academic institution if you finish your studies at the first one or leave the current program with confirmed plans to move to another US institution. Speak to me to help you with the practicalities.

Going home

F-1 visa holders can stay an additional two months in the US after completing their OPT training or academic program.

Should you wish to stay longer and remain in the States, your visa status must be changed: either to another F-1 visa for a new academic venture or to another visa option. You'll need to go through the visa process from the start.

Changing to F-1 status once in the US

Any person with non-immigrant status in the US can apply for a change to F-1 status if such a person has a clean record. (Exceptions are if you are in the US under C, D, K, M, S, TWOV visa categories and in some cases J visas. Speak to me about this.)

There is a lot of documentation needed if you want to apply for a change to F-1 status while you are in the US. You should provide:

- A cover letter explaining why you wish to change to F-1 status.

- Evidence of financial support as discussed before.

- An admission letter from an academic institution.

- Copies of all the relevant USCIS forms (let me help you with this).

- A copy of the receipt from SEVP.

- Copies of all your current immigration documents showing that you are currently in lawful non-immigrant status.

If you are currently in F-2 status: You might be eligible for part-time study. However, shifting to F-1 means that you must be enrolled full-time. If your paperwork is not approved before the start of the next semester, you must stay enrolled part-time in order to maintain F-2 status.

If you are currently in B-1 or B-2 status: You are not allowed to study anywhere until USCIS approves your request.

An alternative method

Alternatively, you can leave the US and freshly apply for an F-1 visa in your home country. If the visa is approved, you can re-enter the US. Your electronic data will be updated from your previous visa, showing your current status as F-1.

2.   O-1 Visa

The definition of the O-1 Visa

The O-1 visa is intended for those individuals with extraordinary ability in the sciences, education, business, athletics, the arts, motion pictures, or television industry.

It is a non-immigrant work visa. You can qualify if you can prove that you've risen to the top of your profession in one of these fields mentioned.

('Arts' can be fine art, culinary art, performing art, or visual art. You can be a set designer, a choreographer, a director, a coach, a makeup artist, or a stage technician. The definition can include any field of work if it can be backed up by the correct documents.)

An O-1 visa holder may travel freely in and out of the US, and there is no cap on the issuing of these visas. Although the requirements for the application are strict, you have a good chance of getting the actual permit.

How long can I stay under an O-1 visa?

This visa can be granted for a specific event, but usually it is valid for three years. The visa can be extended numerous times.

What about my family?

Your wife/husband and children may accompany you to the US under an O-3 visa. They may study in the US but may not work.

Two types of O-1 Visas

- The O-1A visa is for people with outstanding abilities in education, business, science, or athletics.
- The O-1B visa is for individuals in the arts, motion picture, or television industries.

A job offer

To qualify for any of these two visas, the applicant must first have been offered a job from a US employer, referred to as a petitioner. to initiate the visa process.

Evidence, please

The applicant must also provide evidence of his/her extraordinary abilities – either from academic institutions or by sending letters from experts outside of their immediate circle.

The evidence can take on many forms.

For the O-1A visa, look at the following non-exhaustive questions:

- Have you received an Olympic medal?
- A national or international award of excellence in your field?
- Are you a member of a prestige association judged by experts in your field? (It must be an association closed to general members of the public.)
- Were you featured in a high-profile trade magazine or major media newspaper?
- Are you able to judge others in your chosen specialty field, or are you regularly part of a judging panel?
- Are you a published author of a scholarly or technical book or articles?
- Have you made an original contribution of major significance in your field?
- Are you a leader in your field?
- Did you in the past receive a high salary for your skilled service?

For the O-1B visa (motion pictures and television):

You must show evidence that you have been nominated for (or received) an award such as a Golden Globe, an Emmy or an Academy Award (Oscar) OR you can show proof of:

- The fact that you have a lead or starring role in productions and received recognition for it, nationally or internationally.

- This must be backed up with articles in respected journals, newspapers or other publications *about you.*

- You can show box office receipts, motion picture- or television ratings, and more.

- You can prove that you've received a high salary, evidenced by contracts.

- You need a consultation letter from a US peer group, labor organization, and/or management organization. O-1 petitions must include advisory opinions (also called consultation letters) from one of these unions governing their professions in the United States.

- These advisory opinions assist USCIS in assessing the extraordinary talent or essentiality of the beneficiary by enlisting experts in the field to review the petition materials first and provide advice on the eligibility of the person appealing for the visa.

If you can prove any of these (the more, the better!), you have an excellent chance to be approved for an O-1 visa. Contact me for professional guidance to provide this evidence.

Steps to my O-1 Visa

Do you meet the above criteria for an O-1A or O-1B visa? Then, you can begin to prepare your application.

- Your employer or his agent must file Form I-129 with the USCIS office.

- The USCIS will look at all the evidence you submit to prove your status and your answers to the questions listed above.

- Pay the fees and wait for the approval.

- Attend an interview at the US consulate in your country.

It is also possible to change your current visa to O-1 status. However, you must have a valid visa (say, for a tourist or student) and a US employer must be willing to petition for you.

(Let's quickly focus on the distinction between a visa and immigration status. A visa is obtained through a US consulate abroad to enter the country for a specific reason. Immigration status refers to how a person is present in the United States.

So, for example, if a person already in the US changes his or her status from F-1 to O-1 and goes back to his or her county, then he or she has to go to the US consulate to receive an O-1 visa based on O-1 approved status. In the situation when an individual's O-1 petition is approved while waiting in a foreign country, then that person receives an O-1 visa through consular processing.

My area of expertise is petitioners (employers) who seek to help someone obtain O-1 status. I work with beneficiaries seeking the visa to get the correct information from them, which I then carefully tailor to fit the requirements of the permit.

The 'body of evidence'

It is not easy to get an O-1 visa. The 'body of evidence' you need can be very intimidating.

First off, I will chat with you about whether you satisfy the O-1 visa requirements. I will explain to you the process and the investment – not only in terms of finances but also in time and energy.

You must have an extraordinary ability in your field – *and you must be able to prove it.* For some of my clients, this has meant documents of more than 300 pages.

O-1 Visa notes

- I have helped a lot of clients with exceptional abilities in the arts with their O-1 visas. The process is the same for any visa in this category. If you meet the requirements, I can help you.

- It is important to note that you must pay close attention to the requirements listed above. Pertinent information must be sent to immigration services. A personal letter of recommendation emphasizing individual characteristics, for example, is not enough. It is your professional endeavors that must be highlighted.

- A common misperception in connection with this visa is that it can be a guaranteed precursor for an EB-1 visa process (which in turn can lead to a green card.) It is not true. The EB-1 requirements are stricter. An approved O-1 can be a steppingstone for an EB-1 but does not guarantee that you will qualify for the EB-1.

- *A quick comparison between the O-1 visa and the EB-1 visa*

- The O-1 allows for temporary residency. An EB-1 gives you the permanent right to stay in the US.

- The requirements and burden of proof for an EB-1 visa are much more demanding on the applicant.

- You need a sponsor for an O-1 application; not so for an EB-1.

- O-1 visa holder family members cannot work in the US. The dependents of EB-1 holders also get green cards.

- It is possible to go from an O-1 visa holder to a permanent resident in the US. If you want to change your status, you should start early in building a portfolio of your accomplishments in the US. The goal is to be able to prove to USCIS that you are an asset in your field and to America.

- You should file your EB-1 application before your O-1 visa expires. The processing time might take up to a year, less if a lawyer helps you. For an optimized application procedure, ask how I can help you.

- *Please see more information about the EB-1 visa later in this booklet.*

3.   P-1 Visa

The P-1 is another specialty visa, especially for athletes (or other entertainers), their coaches, and support staff.

How to Qualify?

To qualify for a P-1 visa, you must either:

Be internationally recognized as an athlete, and you want to enter the US to compete in an event of **international standing** (the P-1A visa) or,

- You must be part of an outstanding entertainment group who plan to perform in the US (the P-1B visa).

- Coaching and support staff can also get this visa.

To be eligible for the P-1A visa, **athletes** must:

- Be nationally or internationally ranked in a high position and have participated in high-level competitions.

- Obtained a national or international award for excellence.

- Have competed at US sports league level or at a US college or university.

- A letter of recommendation is also needed from appropriate labor unions, as with the O-1 visa.

For the P-1B visa, **entertainers** must:

- Have had significant success in ratings and sales.

- Must have achievements listed in trade journals or major newspapers.

- Be recognized by critics, or other field experts who can testify on their behalf.

- Have received excellent compensation from the activities they do.

To receive a P-1 visa, there must be a US-based sponsor. As a rule of thumb, the team or entertainment group must at least be two persons. A recently formed group will find it hard to qualify.

How long can I stay in the US?

The length of your stay will depend on your competition schedule or your planned performances.

You may be allowed to stay up to five years in the US if you are an individual athlete, but it can be extended to a maximum of ten years.

An athletic team or a group of performers can initially stay for one year, but the visa can be extended by another year, if necessary. Essential personnel can stay initially for one year, but their permission can be extended with another five or even ten years.

It is possible to work for more than one 'employer,' but each one must file a separate petition. An individual or team may change sponsors or employers, but a new request must then be submitted.

Is it possible to get a green card with a P-1 visa?

The P-1 visa is not the friendliest visa to turn into a green card. But it can be done.

What am I allowed to do under a P-1?

- Perform for payment or prize money.

- Study part-time.

- Travel freely in and out of the US.

What about my family?

A spouse and dependent children may accompany the P-1 holder or come and visit under a P-4 visa.

Steps to my P-1 visa

- A US employer or agent must sponsor the group and petition the USCIS (through Form I-129) for approval so that the group can come to the US. Individual performers can also apply but then may only compete or perform on an individual basis. Let me help with this process; it is often complicated.

- Documentation and evidence must be submitted as proof to the requirements outlined above. With my help, it can go smoothly.

- After submission to the USCIS, the process will take between 6–8 weeks.

- Successful groups will receive a Form I-797 and can then start their visa application at their local US embassy.

- Pay the application fee.

- Schedule your interview with the US Embassy. If you are between 14 and 79 years old, it is compulsory.

Like the O-1 visa, a person can also apply for a P-1 visa from abroad or change their current legal non-immigrant status while in the USA to P-1 status.

4.   L-1 Visa

The L-1 is an attractive temporary work visa option. It allows employers to move employees to the US to establish a new branch or office there. Should you be the primary establisher, you'll have one year to get it done. If the company is already up and running, the L-1 visa recipient can qualify for a three-year visa.

There are two types of L-1 visas – an A and a B one. The L-1A visa is issued to a manager to run or start a business in the US. Such a manager can stay in the US for up to seven years.

The L-1B visa is for specialized staff in a company's products, systems, management (and more). The maximum stay for an L-1B visa holder is five years.

If the maximum stay had been reached, the employee must leave the US for one year. After that, the employee can apply again for the same visa.

The L-1 visa is a dual intent visa. It is, therefore, possible for visa holders to become eligible for a green card. An L-1B visa holder can also petition to change their visa to an L-1A.

Can I bring my family?

Yes, L-1 visa holders may bring their families to the US. They will be recipients of the L-2 visa, which runs simultaneously with the L-1 visa. The spouse of the L-1 visa may usually also work without restrictions in the US.

For this booklet, we focus on the L-1A visa as this is the best one for a person to use as a stepping-stone to come and live in the US permanently.

Will I qualify?

The owner of a company who is also the manager (or executive) qualifies for an L-1A visa.

There is no minimum education required for an L-1A visa, which makes it the ideal vehicle for establishing a business in the US.

So, if you've got an existing business with a service or a product that can work well in the US, it may be well worth your while to look at the L-1A visa and how you can expand your business in a foreign country. The company you start may also be a non-profit, a religious, or charitable organization.

It will be essential for you to work with an immigration lawyer if you choose the L-1A visa route. It is not enough just to have the title of a 'manager.' The applicant for this visa must prove that he/she is most definitely a manager or executive within the scope of definitions provided.

This is where I can come in. We must state your case in the best possible way so that it shows that most of your duties are related to the operational management of your business.

The good news is that there is no cap on the number of L-1A visas issued every year. An L-1A visa holder is also allowed to travel back and forth to his/her home country to fulfill work duties.

How to apply for an L-1 visa

- The company fills in a Form 1-129. It is the petition on the employee's behalf. Filing fees must be paid.
- An online form must be filled in.
- The applicant must attend a visa appointment and bring all the required documents so that they can be reviewed.

5.   H-1B Visa

Who can work under an H-1B Visa?

The H-1B visa is a visa issued to specialty occupations.

Per definition, a specialty occupation is a job with duties so specialized that one needs a bachelor's or higher degree to be able to perform. The degree must be typical for the job.

Specialty occupations include graphic designers, fashion designers, journalists, accountants, architects, engineers, doctors, lawyers, business specialists, and various other types of professions.

Should an applicant have at least 12 years of specialized work experience or other qualifications, the bachelor's degree can be bypassed. Therefore, it is also possible for a fashion model to come to the United States under this visa.

In effect, the H-1B visa gives a foreign worker the right to come and work in the US for a US company.

The employer must have been unable to get a US citizen that meets their job requirements and be able to prove it. The employer then sponsors the applicant and pays all the relevant visa fees to bring the worker to the US.

But I was educated in my specialty field in another country

It does not matter. If your education is equivalent to a US bachelor's degree or higher, and the employer is willing to pay a competitive salary, you will most probably pass a credentials evaluation.

What about my family?

The H-1B visa allows family members to join the visa holder for the duration of their stay in the US. Dependent family members (a wife and children under the age of 21) are issued an H-4 visa.

Holders of an H-4 visa can work, go to school, get a driver's license, and even get a social security number. However, the H-4 permits are linked to the primary H-1B visa. Once the primary visa expires, everyone must return to their home country.

How long can I stay in the US under the H-1B visa?

Usually, the visa is valid for up to three years, but it can be extended.

(However, the H-1B visa is a 'dual intent' visa. Holders can also apply for a green card and permanent residency in the US, while they have the H-1B. The sponsoring employer must petition for the change of visa to a green card status through a procession of forms.)

What happens if I quit, get dismissed, or if I want to change jobs?

Your H-1B visa is valid for a fixed employer or job – the one that brought you over to the US in the first place. Should your situation change for any reason, you must go through the visa application process again.

If you find a new job in the US, your new employer must petition for you from scratch.

There is a 60-day grace period to find a new employer, should you quit or be dismissed. If unsuccessful, you must return to your home country.

Steps to my H-1B visa

- *Get sponsored by a US employer to apply.*
- The employer must be willing to help you move to the US. He/she must be aware that you need sponsorship to come to the United States.
- *Employer submits LCA.*

- 'LCA' stands for Labor Condition Application, and it tells the US Department of Labor about the job, its location, pay and working conditions. The employer submits the LCA electronically.

- *Employer submits Form I-129.*

- Once the LCA is approved, the employer must file the USCIS form I-129. All the applicant's supporting documents (such as experience, evaluation documents, training certificates, resume, etc.) and the relevant fees must go with the application. There is a waiting period of 3–4 months for approval.

- *Applicant completes application at US consulate.*

- The last step in the process is for the applicant to process his/her visa at their own country's US embassy or consulate.

All of this may seem daunting. I can help. I will walk with you every step of the way to help you (and your prospective employer if needed) complete the process.

It is not cheap to apply for an H-1B visa. Fortunately, most of the costs of the application will be paid by your new employer.

H-1B visa caps in 2019

For the H-1B visa, there are two pools of permits. Apart from the regular one, you can also apply for an H-1B visa if you have a master's degree in your specialty field.

The cap on the regular pool in 2019 was for 65,000 applications and 20,000 in the master's category. There were almost 100,000 applications in both pools that year.

To resolve the problem, visas were allocated in a lottery. It is expected that this will become the norm in coming years. Everyone, therefore, has a chance of winning a visa. If not selected, candidates can try again in the next fiscal year.

Please keep it mind that compared to other non-immigrant visas, the H-1B may seem somewhat less complicated due to the relatively low eligibility criteria, but the main thing that separates the H-1B from other visas is the annual lottery that takes place. Because of the fact that many more people petition for the H-1B than there are slots available, the USCIS randomly selects 85,000 petitions to be sent to processing. Any that are not selected will have their petitions and fees returned to them.

6.   The E-2 Investor visa

Under the E-2 Treaty Investors visa, an investor can live and work in the United States to develop his business. Unlike the EB-5 visa, this visa does not directly lead to a green card.

Sometimes, in larger businesses, managers are sent to the US under this visa instead of the owners of the company. The investment necessary for this visa varies.

To apply for this visa, the applicant must have realistic plans to establish and fund a business in America.

The investment business should be active and operating. It is expected that employment opportunities should be created for US citizens, much like the EB-5 visa. (However, in this case, there is no set requirement about the number of jobs to be created.)

Part of the investment must be made before applying for E-2 status. It is, therefore, possible to buy a business in the US and then apply for E-2 registration purely based on a purchase agreement.

Much cheaper

The E-2 Treaty Investors visa is worth considering as an alternative to the EB-5 Immigrant Investor green card. There is no need to invest $500,000 or more. Jobs must still be created, but not for a fixed minimum amount.

More aspects of the E-2:

- No cash threshold for investment.

- The investment can include travel, sales, marketing, and equipment purchases.

- You control your own investment and should be involved in the day-to-day running of the business.

- You should employ 2–3 US citizens in your first year or two.

- A business plan must be in place to outline new business plans.

- Documentation with details of qualifications, work history, and skills of workers must be provided.

- The E-2 is a non-immigrant visa category. Upon termination, the principal investor must leave the US.

- However, the visa can be extended indefinitely.

CHAPTER 4
VISAS FOR PERMANENT RESIDENCY

In the previous section, we've discussed temporary visas that may or may not lead to permanent residency. In this section, we are looking at visas that can help you move to the US permanently.

1. Employment-Based Visas

EB visas are also known as employment-based green cards or permanent residency visas. There are a few of these EB visas – each unique.

I can help you to tell them apart. It is essential to be able to choose the right one for your situation. I've helped a lot of immigrants to obtain an EB-1 visa.

The Employment-Based-1 visa

This visa is called the 'Alien of extraordinary ability' visa. It is employment-based.

Does it sound a bit familiar? Yes, the EB-1 visa is like the O-1 visa that we looked at in the previous section. To qualify for both visas, you must show extraordinary skill in your given field, whether it is the sciences, arts, education, athletics, or business.

Unlike the O-1, the EB-1 can be self-petitioned; in other words, a person can file it him- or herself without an employer petitioning for him/her. To involve an employer is not wrong; it can also be done.

What one needs to keep in mind when differentiating between the O-1 and the EB-1 is the **level** of extraordinary skills and its recognition. You need a strategy to evaluate which visa option is the best one for you.

How can I qualify?

There are quite a few routes you can follow.

- Provide evidence that you have an **extraordinary ability** in your field, and your proof must meet at least three of the ten criteria rules set out by the USCIS. A single exceptional accomplishment such as a Grammy Award or the like can also count.

- If you are an outstanding professor or researcher with at least three years' experience and you seek to enter the US to teach or to do further research.

- You've worked for an outside company with a branch in the US for at least one year (within the last three years.) The employer wants you to come to the US in a managerial or executive capacity. You can also be in the US already, working on an L-1 visa.

The good news is that you don't have to show that there are no US workers available to fill the position or fill in a labor certification for this visa.

EB-1 applications are carefully scrutinized and very difficult to obtain. Few people know enough to avoid all the pitfalls. You need an experienced immigration lawyer to help you. I have a track record in securing this type of visa for clients.

I have represented people in this visa classification who were athletes, artists, painters, singers, and scientists. I want to stress this: It is essential to prepare your petition for the EB-1 visa as impeccably as possible.

Often, individuals who are interested in EB-1 are quite famous in their own countries but forget that in America they are not known. You must have enough documentation to show an immigration officer that you really meet the criteria for this visa.

Recommendations from other professionals are good, but more important is your own objective evidence of outstanding abilities.

Other Employment-Based visas

The EB-2 visa: Reserved for highly qualified professionals in a given field with more than five years' experience. The applicant must have a master's degree or higher from a university.

It is different from the EB-1 in the sense that it does not include individuals who have excelled in academics and athletics. If you are a physical therapist, for example, you may qualify for this visa.

You would need an offer of employment and a PERM (Program Electronic Review Management) Labor certification for this visa. (This is not required for the EB-1.)

PERM is the system used for obtaining labor certification and is the first step for certain foreign nationals in obtaining their green cards. The employment-based preference categories that require PERM Labor Certification are EB-2 (other than a National Interest Waiver) and EB-3.

Before a US employer can file an immigration petition for a foreign worker with USCIS, in most EB-2 and EB-3 positions, the employer must first obtain an approved Labor Certification from the Department of Labor (DOL).

An application for labor certification is submitted to the DOL by using ETA Form 9089. The DOL must certify to USCIS that:

- there are not enough US workers able, willing, qualified, and available to accept the job offered the alien at the prevailing wage for that occupation in the area of intended employment, and

- employment of the foreign worker will not adversely affect the wages and working conditions of similarly employed US workers.

The EB-3 visa: Can be obtained by skilled workers with more than two years' experience who can provide a skill not readily available in the US. PERM certification as discussed above is needed.

The EB-4 visa: You can qualify for an EB-4 visa if you are a broadcaster, a NATO employee, an international employee of the US government abroad, a member of the armed forces and more. It is possible to self-petition for this visa, but in most cases, your employer must vouch for you.

The EB-5 visa: The EB-5 is not work-sponsored but is an investor visa. It allows you to live, work, and study in the United States. After five years, you can become eligible for citizenship. It is vital to work with the correct immigration lawyer who can guide you through the steps needed.

In short, by applying for this visa, you are investing in a for-profit US business that qualifies under the EB-5 program. There are minimum capital investment amount requirements that must be met, and the USCIS must approve your application. Typically, applicants for this visa must invest between $500,000 to $1 million into a US commercial enterprise. Mostly, the investments are in real estate or regional centers, but there are also other investments to choose from. Additionally, your investment must be able to create ten full-time jobs for US citizens for two years.

As you can see, the EB-5 visa is different from the other options. The onus is on the investor to make sure that the company they invest in will be able to create the jobs needed to support his/her EB-5 petition.

EB-5 investors are supposed to get their money back over time (some say in 5–6 years.) Yet, there is a risk that it could **not** happen.

However, it is **because** you are willing to take the risk that you are getting permanent resident status in the US. You must work with an immigration lawyer to pick the correct investment (with a proven track record of success) to minimize your risk.

My office can help you by getting all the required documentation together. It will include tax returns, bank statements, employment records, and more. It can take up to two years for an applicant for an EB-5 visa to receive their green card. It is, therefore, a visa that needs some strategy – which I can provide.

2.   Family-based Green Cards

A marriage green card

What is a marriage-based green card?

Should an immigrant get married to a US citizen, a marriage-based green card allows the person to live and work anywhere in the United States.

It is not yet US citizenship. The green cardholder will have permanent resident status and can apply for citizenship after three years.

There are three steps to this green card:

- You must be legally married. You must submit your marriage certificate.
- Apply for the green card.
- Attend an interview and wait on the result.

I can help you with this application. It is not that difficult, but there can be details unique to your situation that we have to anticipate and plan for. I will help you prepare for your marriage green card interview and tell you about the questions that are likely to be asked.

Most importantly, your marriage must be genuine. You will not be eligible for the green card if you cannot convince the immigration officer that your spouse really married you for love. USCIS will get suspicious if you are not living in the same house, not speaking the same language, or come from extremely different backgrounds.

The US citizen must be willing to sponsor the immigrant for years

A US citizen can petition for his parents, children, or stepchildren

Children

A US Citizen can also petition for children or stepchildren. He/she must be willing to support the children. Most likely, children will get green cards together with their mother/father if they are unmarried and not yet 21.

Immediate relatives are given high priority under immigration laws. Each would need a separate visa petition, however.

Married children and children over 21 are not automatically eligible for a visa. It is possible for them to get it based on the US spouse, but not a given.

Parents

Reach out to me if you want to know how to sponsor your parents to come to the US and live here permanently. It can be complicated, and you would need my experience.

According to the USCIS, you must be US citizen yourself and at least 21 years old to sponsor your parents. If you are only a green card holder yourself, you may not submit a petition to bring your parents to the US.

Separate petitions must be filed for each of your parents. Supporting documents showing the family relationship must accompany it.

If your parents were not married at the time you were born or did not get married before you were 18, the procedure is different. You would need to provide more evidence of the parent-child relationship. Speak to me about how I can help.

If your I-130 petition is approved, your parents' cases will be referred to the National Visa Center. The Center will collect fees and more supporting documents. During this processing, you must be able to prove that you will be able to support your parents financially, should they come to the US.

The last step is an interview at your local consulate before the visa processing can be completed.

♦ ♦ ♦

CHAPTER 5
PERMANENT RESIDENCY THROUGH THE VIOLENCE AGAINST WOMEN'S ACT

There are other ways to get permanent residency to live and work in the United States. I feel it must be added here to give you the complete picture.

VAWA - The Violence Against Women Act

Immigrants can benefit from the VAWA. If you are a spouse, parent, or child of a US citizen and have been a victim of abuse, you may self-petition for a green card. You won't have to rely on the abuser anymore to obtain lawful status in the United States.

Let me help you to find out if you are eligible for a green card under the VAWA.

A short history of the VAWA

Why such an act?

Over the decades, the crime rate in the US was rising. Not only this, but its primary victims were women. The violent crime rate in America doubled between 1960 and 1970, igniting concerns from the public, but also government officials. Something had to give.

Researchers collected more data, and as a result, family violence was re-classified from being a private family matter to a crime.

In 1984, President Reagan enacted the Family Violence Prevention and Services Act (FVPSA). Its big brother, the 'Violent Crime Control and Law Enforcement Act,' came in 1994, signed by President Clinton. The Violence Against Women Act (VAWA) is part of it as Title IV.

VAWA is, therefore, part of another larger violent crime control act. It was created primarily to protect women, and it envisioned a change in attitude towards violence against women.

Since then, VAWA has been reauthorized and expanded four times (in 2000, 2005, 2013, and 2019) to add human trafficking, sex trafficking, issues about American Indian tribal laws, backlogs in rape cases, date rape, battering, and stalking.

Office on Violence Against Women (OVW)

VAWA was created to protect women against violent abuse. An office was opened within the US Department of Justice to deal with VAWA cases, implement legislation, and administer grant programs.

The grants are to prevent and address domestic violence or abuse. Shelters can get funds here, as well as programs that can educate and train. OVW also organizes government funding for studies on abuse against women.

A watershed bill

For the first time, there was now an act designed to end violence against women. VAWA is the first comprehensive federal legislative package to address this. It was a triumph for numerous women's groups who fought for the law to be passed. They said that previously, the state did not address this adequately.

It was not easy

The passing of the act did not come without opposition. It took four years to go through the channels because it also allowed victims to sue their attackers.

The opposition argued that family disputes would flood the courts if this specific provision were allowed. In the end, the wording of the regulation was carefully redrafted until it was perfect to meet with everyone's approval.

A new conversation

The VAWA sparked conversation about abuse and violence. A woman in a crisis, without any resources and whose life is in danger, can now get help. The OVW funds (and requires from its grant programs) a coordinated community response to violence.

One of the biggest problems is housing. If someone wants to break free from domestic violence, she must be able to leave – to go somewhere where she and her children will be safe. Often, this is the one thing that will keep a woman from leaving her abuser. VAWA and the OVW help.

But, what does the VAWA entail exactly?

The Violence Against Women Act of 1994 has three main areas of competence:

- The investigation and prosecution of sex offenses, mainly against women,
- The provision of several grant programs, and

- Immigrant provisions for abused aliens.

For the purpose of this booklet, we will focus on the third area. But, before we zoom in, just a quick overview of the first two VAWA areas of competence.

To investigate and to prosecute

The very first intention of the VAWA was to make a difference in cases where violence against women was the problem.

- New offenses and penalties were created, for instance, where a protection order was violated or where an abuser crossed a state line to injure someone.

- VAWA forces states and counties to enforce protection orders issued by *other* countries.

- Repeat sex offenders now face harsher sentences. Under VAWA, probation officers are also trained to know how to handle these offenders.

- Rules of evidence were modified, confidentiality issues addressed in domestic violence cases, and restitution to victims of sexual abuse installed.

- Rape victims can demand HIV tests from alleged assailants.

Grants

The original VAWA created a host of grant programs. These were:

- Preventative grants to avoid assault.

- Collaboration grants between different role players.

- Grants for investigation and prosecuting domestic violence-related crimes.

- Grants that underline the seriousness of these crimes.

- Grants especially for rural states.

- Grants to prevent crimes on public transportation or in parks.

With the expansion of the act, more grants were added. To name a few:

- Grants for youth education on domestic violence.

- Grants for community intervention and prevention programs.

- A National Domestic Violence Hotline was created, and funding organized to build shelters for battered women.

VAWA reached far and wide. It changed the landscape of domestic- and intimate partner violence. VAWA is also an act for immigrants.

Immigration provisions

Of course, domestic violence and crime occur at all levels of our society. Just because someone is an immigrant, it does not mean the person would not have the same problems as their US counterparts.

The 1994, VAWA included three provisions related to abused aliens:

- A provision for self-petitioning by abused foreign national spouses. (This allows someone to get her own lawful status in the place of status that depended on the sponsorship of an abusive spouse.)

- Battered spouse waivers, and

- Cancellation of deportation under VAWA for abused spouses and their children.

(I'll explain each of these options in more detail below.) But first...

Why do immigrants need the VAWA?

The following scenario is a genuine one for thousands of immigrant women (and men).

The not so perfect love story

You meet the man of your dreams in your home country. He is a US citizen on a visit, and he sweeps you off your feet. Then, not long afterward comes a marriage proposal. He convinces you to go with him to the US on a fiancé visa, leaving your friends and family behind.

Once you're married, things change drastically. The man you thought loved you is suddenly rude and abusive. Some women are forced to do things against their will.

You are trapped. You don't speak English. Your immigration status prevents you from getting a job or even a driver's license. Some women are forced to live in remote places. They must rely on their husbands to be their driver, translator, and provider.

As a foreign spouse of a US citizen, you are entitled to apply for a green card eventually. But what if your husband refuses? This is not uncommon.

Why don't these women just go home?

Abusers often use the victim's immigration status as a tool to get them to stay. The abuser might also limit the victim's contact with other people, discourage friendships, and demean her because she struggles with settling in the US.

Outside influences can also play a role in preventing these women from leaving. In some cultures, domestic violence is seen as something very private. You must keep quiet. What would your family say?

Intimate partner violence is terrible. Even though some inroads have been made, there is still an urgent need to develop programs to help immigrant women. Prevention (or even early intervention) is always better than cure!

There is a way out

Immigrants are often unaware that there **are** options available to them. They end up staying in an abusive home because they don't know what else to do. They might fear deportation. They receive no help from social services.

The VAWA opened up legal options for these people. Immigrant victims of abuse are now able to adjust their immigration status to permanent status. VAWA protects them.

For someone who was battered, this means she can stay in the US legally, **without** having to depend on the abuser to vouch for her. Such a victim can self-petition (for herself and her children) and receive a green card. The spouse need not even to know about it as the entire process is anonymous.

In 2017, more than 3,000 self-petition applications were granted by the USCIS for foreign victims of spousal abuse. Because of the VAWA, immigrant women now have the same civil and criminal law protection as American citizens.

What type of abuse is covered by the act?

VAWA's emphasis is on women. The original passage of the act was because of the public concern over violence against women. (Today, men and children are also covered through the provisions of VAWA.) All this, of course, is also true for immigrant men.

VAWA has a range of programs that address sexual assault, stalking, dating violence, and domestic violence. The programs state how the criminal justice system can 'help,' but also mobilize community response and involvement. Specific programs focus on preventive measures.

What follows is a summary of different types of abuse that are legally covered by VAWA.

Physical violence

Physical violence can also be described as 'battery.' Kicking, punching, slapping, and boxing are all examples of battery. The victim is physically hurt. Some abusers use all sorts of devices to hit the victim.

Verbal abuse

Verbal abuse can be just as hurtful as physical violence. Verbal abuse can range from mere insults to yelling and screaming daily.

Example: One abuser called his wife every despicable name under the sun and tried to put her down at every opportunity. He even yelled at her if there was water in the sink after she had done the dishes. He yelled and cursed at anything that was not the way he liked it.

Threats of harm

Under VAWA, the violence or threats of violence need not be limited to only immediate family. Sometimes abusers cause trouble for (or threaten to harm) other family or friends, or even pets.

Example: In one of my cases, the abuser would get infuriated over small things. The victim was always walking on eggshells. She was afraid of what would happen if she did anything wrong. When the abuser was driving the car while angry at her, he would drive very fast and violently, aiming to scare her.

Abuse of a sexual nature

Forms of sexual abuse include force (including threats of force), and unwanted sexual behavior. Sexual abuse can also count as a battery or extreme cruelty under VAWA. The definitions here also include forced sexual activity with others (prostitution.)

Intimidation

This heading could have read 'degradation' or 'humiliation' too. The victim fears the consequences if they dare to go against the abuser.

The abuser can intimidate by:

- Making fun of the victim in public.
- Giving stern, warning looks.
- Clenching fists or displaying a weapon.
- Standing very close to the victim.
- Threatening to call the authorities to deport the victim.

All these are recognized grounds for victims to seek protection under VAWA.

Isolation or 'jailing' the victim

Imagine it: a new culture, a new home, and a new language. It can be intimidating for even the strongest person. Immigrants are especially vulnerable. They are already unsure of themselves, and it is therefore elementary for an abuser to isolate his victim socially.

The abuser can:

- Refuse to let the victim call friends or family.
- Tell the victim whom she can see or cannot see.
- Refuse to let her drive.
- Refuse to let her leave the house to mingle and go to social activities.

In some cases, the abuser is effectively 'jailing' the victim and isolating her from everything and everyone. VAWA also has remedies for this.

Economic abuse

Economic abuse can take various forms. The victim might not have her own money, and the abuser refuses to give her any. He doesn't let her have a job. In extreme cases, abusers might even take action to get a woman fired from a current position to gain more control over her. Some abusers stalk or harass their spouse at work to get them to quit or to be fired.

Example: Susan (not her real name) had to supply the money for her husband to do the grocery shopping. He would never offer any money but would wait to see if she would buy the groceries herself. When she dared to ask about his financial situation, he would not respond or get very angry.

Jealousy harassment

Some immigrant spouses become incredibly jealous of their wives. They accuse them of infidelity and flirting with other men. Actions recognized by VAWA in this regard are:

- Going through the victim's mail or email.
- Checking up continuously on the person at home or work.
- Trying to solicit friends, family, and even employers for information about the victim's habits.
- Following the person.

This humiliates the victim and causes embarrassment.

Example: One of my clients reported that her abuser was always paranoid about her fidelity and accused her of seeing other men. He tortured her by always questioning her about her whereabouts. Any unusual mark on her body was evidence to him that she was touched by another man.

Immigration control

One of the very reasons for VAWA to come into being was the fact that abusers control victims by using their immigration status. 'If you don't do what I say, I will get you deported. You won't be able to take the children!'

Abusers lie to their victims. They tell them that they don't have any rights to social services in the US, for example. They also explain to them that the police and the courts won't protect them.

Example: I see this a lot in my cases. The abuser tells the victim that she would not be able to report his behavior as he would 'get her deported.'

In conclusion

As all of this is untrue, there needed to be some or other way to start protecting these victims. VAWA recognizes all these forms of abuse and gives victims a way to get out of a toxic relationship.

Now you know what types of abuse are recognized under VAWA, you can examine your situation. Perhaps you never even thought or knew that you have rights. You no longer need to suffer from an abusive person. VAWA was created for people like you.

In the next section, I'll discuss the options open to you and how I can help you.

How can I help you? – General comments

I want to spend a little time to tell you the procedure once you contact me to help you. It might help to make you feel less unsure of what would happen.

- First, when we meet, I would want to make sure that you are safe and feel safe then. If not, there are community resources that we can turn to. It will be my very first priority. We cannot talk about generalities if you feel that your life might be in danger. We shall address that first. Should you need police involvement, we can discuss that too.

- At the very least, we can make a safety plan. I can help you assess your situation, and we can decide what you should do the next time you feel unsafe or as if your life is threatened.

- I shall ask you if you need any medical attention immediately. If so, we'll attend to it. I'd be happy to tell you about possible resources open to you in this regard, should you need it in the future. We sincerely hope that it would not come to that!

- I shall ask you if you are comfortable to converse in English. If not, it is no problem. I speak Georgian and Russian fluently. If needed, we can get an interpreter to help.

Identifying your immigration status

I know that this can be a sensitive issue for you. You might fear deportation – if not for yourself, maybe for your children or even for your abuser.

You may be afraid that you will lose:

- Access or custody to your children.
- Your status to be in the US and never see your children again.
- The ability to provide financially for the family at home.
- Friends and family in general if you leave your abuser.

You must understand: your abuser cannot take away your current legal status. If you have a current, valid visa, you (or your children) will not be deported.

(The only exceptions are if you fraudulently entered the US, violated conditions of your visa, or were convicted of a crime.)

I would need to know your immigration status to best help you. I will keep it confidential. Knowing your status will help me to assess if you might need immediate legal representation.

Don't worry. Whatever your immigration status is, I shall still help you. I won't leave you because of an administrative issue.

What options do you have under the VAWA?

Immediate help

To summarize, there are a lot of immediate options available to you that can alleviate your situation.

I'd be happy to tell you about emergency medical care and crime victim services, police assistance, how your abuser can be prosecuted, funds that you might have access to, emergency shelters in your area, and how a protection order works. There are public benefits for the children of US citizens, as well as child support options.

You are no longer alone. The regulators of the VAWA already thought of every possible situation.

Once we've made sure that we've covered your immediate situation and that you feel safe, we can move on to the legalities of your situation. There are relevant immigration laws that apply to your situation. Once I know your immigration status and your story, I can help with this.

Five possible ways to get help under the VAWA

The VAWA offers you relief and a host of services.

To summarize, you can self-petition under the VAWA, you can receive a battered spouse waiver, or you can apply for a 'cancellation of deportation.'

It is also possible to apply for a U-visa or a T-visa.

Let's look at each of the legal options available to you under this act.

Self-petitioning under the VAWA

What you should know about self-petitioning

- This section of the VAWA applies to abused immigrants who are married to a US citizen (or someone who is a lawful permanent resident of the country.) The US citizen can also be your child ('elder abuse.')

- 'Self-petitioning' means that you don't need your husband or family member to do anything for you to get legal status in the US. You can file your own petition. With it, you seek the adjustment of your legal situation. You can also request that your filing fees be waived.

Who exactly can self-petition?

- A spouse or a divorced spouse. (Here you must file within two years, and the termination of the marriage must be due to the abuse that the victim suffered.)

- Children under 25 years of age.

- An immigrant parent of an abused child, even if he/she was not harmed in itself.

To use this option, you must be able to show the following:

- Evidence of the fact that you live with your abuser.

- You were abused. You must document evidence of abuse.

- You must show that your marriage was entered into in good faith.

- You must be of good standing and have solid moral values.

- Your immigration status.

- Parent-child relationship if applying for a child.

It can be daunting to create this body of evidence. Don't worry. I will walk you through it all.

I don't have any documents

Another problem is that some self-petitioners may find it hard to gather the evidence needed. They might not be living at home anymore, or their husband is the only one who has access to documents.

The good news is that the USCIS will accept more 'informal' evidence such as letters or signed affidavits from self-petitioners. The only thing that matters is that your documents are believable. (The standard that the USCIS uses is the 'any credible evidence' standard.)

I suggest you keep track of your efforts to get the documents you need. For example, if you tried a few times to get a police report from a domestic violence incident and get rejected because you don't have identification, write down the effort you have made and why you were denied. It is also acceptable for a friend who saw the abuse you've suffered to write a letter.

Don't worry about the body of evidence. Because of the any 'credible evidence standard,' we can get resourceful, and I can help you with gathering relevant documentation.

If approved, your VAWA self-petition will mean that you will be able to work in the US and apply for lawful permanent residency.

Self-petitioning can be complicated. For example, it is also possible to apply as a derivative family member of an approved VAWA self-petitioner. I can help you with more information about this and about what the eligibility criteria are.

Battered spouse waivers

A battered spouse waiver is available to immigrants with conditional residency. 'Conditional residency' is a temporary two-year green card issued to prevent marriage fraud. Usually, the legal resident spouse applied for this green card in the first place.

After two years, full lawful permanent residency may be granted to the immigrant.

What happens if the abused victims feel compelled to remain in the relationship to get their green card. Two years can be a really long time!

The 'battered spouse waiver' was created under the VAWA so that domestic violence victims can remove their conditional status if they can prove battery or extreme cruelty. It must be shown too that the marriage was valid in the first place.

What will happen here is that the 'conditional stay' will be removed, and the battered spouse will be able to apply for permanent residency. Her abuser need not know or participate in the process at all.

Who can file?

- A battered spouse
- Her children
- A widow or divorcee who will be subjected to extreme hardship if she was made to return to her home country.

How this differs from VAWA self-petition

Your current stay in the US must be **conditional** on applying for a battered spouse waiver. You have a temporary green card. For the VAWA self-petition, you don't have any legal status yet.

How to prove battery and 'extreme cruelty' for this waiver.

Battery is physical violence. Slapping, punching, pushing, or any other infliction of injury on your body (including non-consensual sex) are considered 'battery.'

'Extreme cruelty' is defined by the USCIS as intentional, non-violent abuse intended to control, dominate, or humiliate.

Some examples include:

- Threatening to report you to the USCIS or any other government agency.
- Threatening divorce.
- Controlling you by managing phone calls, computer usage, and more.
- Withholding money or food from you.
- Destroying your personal property.

If you contact me, we will need to prove how your spouse has been abusive and how he hurt and controlled your life. It can be a painful and emotional journey. Unfortunately, if you want to stay in the US, it is necessary to show this to the USCIS so that you can get a waiver and, ultimately, a green card.

I will help you with instructions on how to fill in the relevant forms and what to file with the USCIS.

In short, along with your petition, you must be able to provide:

- A filing fee.
- A copy of your permanent residency card.
- Evidence of battery or extreme cruelty.
- Proof that your marriage was not a 'sham' but genuine.

What will happen next?

Under the VAWA 'battered spouse waiver', you will receive a receipt that will serve as your 'green card' while your case is being reviewed. You won't have to leave the US, but you may continue to live and work there.

USCIS might send you some requests for evidence. Respond to them in a timely way.

Eventually, you will be invited for an interview at a USCIS office to discuss all the particulars of your case.

Cancellation of deportation under the VAWA

The VAWA 'cancellation of removal' is a form of relief. It was designed to keep victims in abusive relationships from being deported.

A non-citizen can turn to the immigration court after being placed in removal proceedings. If successful, this would mean that lawful permanent resident status can be obtained – also for children.

To qualify for cancellation of deportation under the VAWA, a victim must prove quite a few things:

- She has lived in the US for at least three years, and she has an excellent moral character.

- If forced to leave the US, it will cause extreme hardship for the victim herself, her children, or a parent.

- She had been battered or subjected to extreme hardship by a US citizen spouse or parent.

- Marriage fraud will automatically make such a victim ineligible for cancellation, as well as if convicted of an aggravated felony.

The definitions for battery and 'extreme cruelty' under this heading are much the same as in the other sections. To summarize, it can be any act (or threatened act) of violence, psychological or sexual abuse, or acts that constitute an overall pattern of violence.

Physical presence in the US

The cancellation of deportation under the VAWA calls for the victim to have maintained a presence in the US for three years. During these three years, the victim may not have been out of the country for longer than 90 days in once stretch, or absent in access of 180 days in total over the whole three years. However, this requirement is subject to review if it can be proved that your absences were connected to the abuse at the hand of the US spouse or parent.

Hardship if removed

The applicant to this section of the VAWA must show that extreme hardship would occur if he/she were removed from the US. It can be personal, or the misfortune could 'happen' to a child or a parent.

Regulations explain that deportation will only be avoided if the applicant can show one or more of the following:

- The extent and nature of the consequences of abuse.
- How **not** having access to the US courts will impact the victim.
- The likelihood of retaliation of the batterer's family or friends.
- That a child needs some medical, mental health or social need that is unavailable in the home country.
- How domestic violence is seen in the home country. Some applicants may be punished **because** they were victims.
- The abuser can freely travel, and the applicant (and her children) will not be protected in the home country.

Discretionary

It must be noted here that the cancellation of deportation is totally discretionary, and an immigration judge will take all the facts into account. It is not to say that cancellation of removal will take place automatically, even if the applicant meets all the requirements.

It will be well worth your while to consult with me first for a full evaluation of your particular situation. I shall tell you about all the remedies that might be available to you.

A VAWA green card – how can you get one?

Despite the name of the law, VAWA can apply to any petitioner, male or female. To obtain your green card, you must be able to prove the following:

1. The legal status of the abuser

Your relative must be a US citizen or a lawful permanent resident. You can still file a petition under VAWA if the abuse occurred **before** the person gained citizenship, or even if the abuser lost their permanent residence. Then, however, your request must be filed within two years.

2. You are a spouse, child, or parent of the abuser

You could obtain a VAWA green card even if your marriage ended because of abuse. (You must just make sure that you apply within two years after the marriage ended.) Children under 21 years of age can be included in your self-petition. Parents can also apply if battered in any way by a United States citizen.

3. An abusive relationship

The petitioner for a VAWA green card must be able to show that he/she had been battered or was subjected to extreme cruelty.

The battery can include physical violence and/or sexual abuse.

Extreme cruelty behaviors include emotional abuse, threats to harm you, controlling behavior, or keeping you locked up against your will.

These examples are not exhaustive. The USCIS will consider the totality of your unique circumstances before deciding.

4. A good faith marriage

Your marriage to the abuser must have been genuine and not entered to obtain a green card.

5. Do you live in the US?

To file a VAWA petition, you must reside in the US. There are some exceptions, such as when the abuser is an employee of the US government or armed services or if the abuse occurred within the US, but you are not currently living there.

You must have lived with the abuser at some point, although VAWA does not specify for how long.

6. A person of good standing

You can only apply for a VAWA green card if you can show that you have no criminal history, that you are not an alcoholic, using drugs, are not gambling or harming anyone else. You must be clean from any of these behaviors for at least three years.

I have had a lot of clients with VAWA issues in the past. I can help. We would need to demonstrate that you've been abused and that you qualify for a VAWA green card under the requirements mentioned above. I can send you to a psychologist to affirm extreme cruelty.

◆ ◆ ◆

CHAPTER 6
THE U-VISA AND THE T-VISA

Up to here, we've discussed three options you have to receive a permanent green card to the US under the VAWA.

But there are two more visa options that we should discuss. The 'U' and the 'T' visas were both created to encourage victims of serious crimes to work with the police to catch perpetrators.

1.   The U-visa

What is the U-visa?

The U-visa allows victims of certain types of crimes to get a temporary non-immigrant visa and a work permit to the US. Eventually, such a person can get a green card.

There are three requirements:

- You must be a victim of a qualifying crime.
- You must have suffered much because of the crime and,
- You must be helpful while the crime is being investigated.
- Part of the reasoning here is that if an immigrant stays in the

country, US law enforcement will have access to the information they need to solve a crime. The carrot of permanent residency makes it easier to convince witnesses to testify in serious crimes.

This is relevant under the VAWA because sexual abuse and domestic violence also are qualifying crimes. (Some other qualifying crimes include abduction, extortion, prostitution, rape, false imprisonment, stalking, and more.)

I will help to identify if you might qualify for a U-visa. We would need to fill in all the forms and provide documentation and supporting evidence for our stance. However, you must know that there is a very long waiting list to be granted a U-visa. Recently, USCIS changed the rules. It is now possible to get temporary residency status while you wait for your U-visa.

Who can qualify?

Any foreign national who suffered physical or mental abuse as a victim of a qualifying crime can qualify for a U-visa. The crime must have happened somewhere within the US. Should you want to apply for this visa, you must be able to prove that you were the victim of a major crime.

Please note that the applicant for the U-visa must be the **direct** victim of the crime. (There are some exceptions, such as when the direct victim was murdered, and family members can help the police or where a bystander to a violent crime can offer invaluable information.)

You would need a certificate from an approved government agency. The document is called a 'Certification of Helpfulness.' To receive it, you must be able to fulfill the three requirements mentioned already. (You were a victim, you suffered, and you want to help the government.)

The main requirement here is **how much** you've suffered. The USCIS would want medical and legal documents to support your claims. They will consider the amount of suffering, how it damaged you, and for how long.

The certification can come from any federal or state authority that routinely investigates or prosecutes criminal activity. The reason for this is mainly to prevent immigration fraud. Possible certifying agencies include federal or state agencies, child protection services, the Department of Labor, local law enforcement agencies, prosecutors, or judges.

How does it work?

- I will help you to petition for your U-visa. We submit supporting evidence to the USCIS.

- The USCIS will evaluate each case by its merits. They will not be bound by previous decisions for other immigration benefits.

- If successful, you will receive a U-visa. It is temporary for a non-immigrant, and it will allow you to stay in the US for up to four years. The visa may even be extended if a law enforcement agency confirms that the investigation is still pending, and the visa holder is still needed to assist with a prosecution.

- Should your application be denied, we will be notified in writing. An appeal is possible.

- After three years in the US, a U-visa holder can apply for a green card.

Conditions to switch to a green card

- You must have been available to the criminal investigation throughout.

- You must prove that your need to stay in the US is due to a humanitarian need or will promote the unity of your family.

The benefit of a U-visa, therefore, is that you can work in the US and apply for a green card eventually. Authorization can be extended to family members, too. The U-2 to U-5 visas are allocated to spouses, children, parents, and minor siblings, respectively.

To apply for the green card, you must still be under U-status. The conditions stated above are the basics. More documents need to be submitted. I can help you with this.

Immigrant women as victims

Immigrant women are especially vulnerable to violence. They often stay in abusive relationships because they are afraid of being reported to the authorities.

The U-visa is, therefore, another 'out' for these victims. Research has shown this visa as an essential tool in helping law enforcement to strengthen relationships in immigrant communities. Members are now more comfortable in reporting crimes.

2.   The T-visa

The definition of the T-visa

The very aptly named T-visa was brought into being to provide immigration relief to victims of human trafficking.

Human trafficking can also be translated as 'modern-day slavery' in different forms. Victims are often promised the moon and the stars but are then rudely awakened when they arrive in the US.

The definition of 'human trafficking' includes:

> Sex trafficking where the sex act is induced by fraud or force (or where the victim is younger than 18) or the recruitment of someone through fraud to be a slave to someone else.

The T-visa helps these people by letting them stay in the US. They get permission to work and have access to social services. Part of the reason for allowing them to remain, of course, is to assist in subsequent investigations.

The 'Certification of Helpfulness' is not necessary under T-visa as it is under the U-visa. However, a declaration from a law enforcement agency that you were a victim of human trafficking would be beneficial in your application for a T-visa.

What qualifies as human trafficking under the T-visa?

Human trafficking can be explained in three words:

Process: It is the recruitment, transportation, harboring or receiving of someone.

Way: by threat, abduction, fraud, deception.

To: use for sexual exploitation, prostitution, slavery.

Let's look at this example: A woman was recruited to come to the US and 'work' as a nanny. Her passport is taken away on arrival, and she is forced to work as a nanny without pay. She is a victim of human trafficking because she was recruited by deception and is now forced to work as a slave.

To qualify for a T-visa, your presence in the US must be due to human trafficking. If not for the actions of another person, you would not be here.

Who can qualify?

- You must be a direct victim of human trafficking, according to the above definitions.

- You must be physically present in the US, American Samoa,

or the Northern Mariana Islands. It is not possible to apply for a T-visa outside of the US at another consulate.

- You must be willing to assist the police and other law enforcement officials in capturing your traffickers. If you are under 18, you may be exempt from this requirement.

- You must demonstrate that you will suffer and come to harm if removed from the US.

The validity of a T-visa

A T-visa can be valid for up to four years. You can apply for a green card after three years. Family members can also stay in the US if they qualify.

The sad face of the T-visa

It is hard to know exactly how many people are trafficked into the US every year, although estimates suggest that about 50,000 people are trafficked into the US each year, most often from Mexico and the Philippines, but other countries too.

The crime is underreported. Why?

Victims are working, their wages are being withheld, and they are not allowed to leave. They are made to work incredible hours. How can they get free?

Language barriers and isolation keep victims away from help. Some don't even understand what happened to them or that help is available. They just want to survive and are afraid to ask for help.

You must know that this option of the T-visa is available to you under the VAWA. It may be hard to obtain, but I can help.

◆ ◆ ◆

CHAPTER 7
SEEKING REFUGE OR ASYLUM
IN THE UNITED STATES

As a lawyer, I also specialize in helping people to gain refugee or asylum status. I can help you prove your case to the US government. Refugees must apply from outside the US, whereas people requesting asylum can apply at a US border or from within the US.

There is a condition to become a refugee or asylee: You must fear for your safety and the fact that you are being persecuted based on either race, religion, nationality, group, or political views.

Let's look at refugees first.

Refugee status

What is a refugee?

Gloria was one

Gloria Estefan, the famous singer, and songwriter, was born in Havana in 1957. Her family fled Cuba when Fidel Castro took power, and they made a new life in the US. Gloria joined a band in her twenties and moved up the ranks until her 1984 album *Eyes of Innocence* rocked the charts. The rest is history!

Definition of a refugee

A refugee is someone who does not live within the US but has a humanitarian reason to come to the US. You must be able to demonstrate that you fear persecution in some way in your country. It can be due to religion, political opinion, race, and more.

In Gloria's situation, her father was a Cuban soldier who feared for his life under communist Fidel Castro.

To gain refugee status in the US, you must also not already be settled in another country, and you must be admissible. You cannot, in any way, be someone who ordered the persecution of anyone else. So, if you participated in war crimes or terrorism yourself, you are excluded from protection and cannot gain refugee status in the US.

Refugees are anyone (men, women, and children) fleeing war, political upheaval, or oppression. They are seeking safety in another country. Usually, they must flee without warning and do so quickly. Because of their fear, their own country is not a safe place for them to be anymore.

Refugees in the US - a few facts

- There is a new set of rules in place for refugee admissions in 2020. Under the Trump administration, a cap of 18,000 refugees in 2020 is planned. This is almost half of those admitted in the fiscal year that ended on 30 September 2019.

- The number of refugees allowed has been steadily declining since 2016. In the 2016-2017 year, the cap was just over 50,000 refugees.

- After 9/11, the US allowed remarkably fewer refugees to

enter the country. In 2019, most refugees came from Burma, then Ukraine, and Eritrea.

- Most refugees eventually settle in New York, Texas, Washington, or California.

- Overall, most Americans believe that the country has some responsibility in allowing refugees to come to the Land of the Free.

See more key facts about refugees to the US here:

www.pewresearch.org/fact-tank/2019/10/07/key-facts-about-refugees-to-the-u-s/

Not that easy to apply

The fact of the matter is that it is not that easy to get refugee status anymore. I must be honest with you about it. The process can be a long one, and you would need support to be successful.

You cannot 'apply' to become a refugee. You must get a referral, and even then, it is not guaranteed that you will be given refugee status.

Once classified as a refugee, though, there are agencies within the US that will give you support. I'd be happy to consult with you about your options.

The process of becoming a refugee

1. First, a referral

To get refugee status, a referral is needed. Your reference can come from the United Nations High Commission for Refugees (UNHCR), a US embassy, or a non-governmental organization. The referral will be assessed by the United States Refugee Admissions Program (USRAP).

Role of the USRAP

Every year, the law dictates that the USRAP look at the overall world-wide refugee situation. They must predict how the US can help in the possible resettling of refugees.

They set out the 'reasons' that applicants can use to justify humanitarian issues.

After much discussion with various parties, this document is signed by the President of the US. The Presidential Determinations states how many people will be admitted to the US as refugees and from where. Particular humanitarian concerns are addressed every year by the panel.

For instance, in 2019, priorities were:

- Cases identified and referred to the USRAP by the United Nations High Commissioner for Refugees, a US embassy, or an NGO.
- Special humanitarian groups as identified by the US Refugee Admissions Program.
- Cases where families can be reunited.

2. Referral accepted

Once your referral has been accepted by the USRAP, you'll be asked for details. (Remember, USRAP is part of the US State Department. The USRAP is the program that manages the whole process for refugees.)

Now you must present your documentation, and you are initially screened. You will be referred to a US State Department Resettlement Support Centre (RSC). There are nine around the world. You must be able to provide proof of persecution and be able to tell why you are afraid to return to your home country. Your affidavit must be very detailed to be considered.

Officials from RSC's will interview you and look at your data. A background check will also be done on your criminal record, past immigration violations, and possible connection to terrorist groups. Some potential refugees will be subjected to medical tests. You might be denied as a refugee for polygamy, smuggling, or previous deportations. Individuals from 'high-risk' countries are also screened.

This whole process can take up to two years to complete.

You may include your spouse and children under the age of 21 (and unmarried) in your case. Generally, the USCIS will look at where you got married to see if it is valid for immigration law purposes.

There is no fee to be paid to 'apply' for refugee status. The information you share will not be revealed in any way to your home country.

An overseas USCIS officer will decide your fate. If approved, you will be given a visa for refugee resettlement.

A private voluntary agency will help decide where you will live. You don't need a sponsor to come to the US, but if you do have a relative living in the country, efforts will be made to place you near that person.

Eventually, your travel to the US will be scheduled and arranged. You will be given an interest-free loan on your travel costs, which must be paid back to the US within six months of you being in the US.

Coming to the US as a refugee

What will happen once you come to the US?

There's good news! Once you come to the US as a refugee, there are many agencies ready to give you support. Housing? They will help. They will also discuss employment options with you, help with access to English language classes, and more. These are unique benefits to refugees that are not available to asylum seekers.

Benefits once you arrive in the US

There is a particular US office that helps refugees. It is called the ORR

(Office of Refugee Resettlement). This office works with various other non-profits and will help you with one or more of the following:

- Finding a place to live and furnishing it.

- Helping you to understand how the local transportation system works.

- Getting your children into a school.

- Helping you to find a job.

- Helping to show you how to use services such as going to a doctor or learning English.

You might be eligible for medical- or cash assistance from your state government. It is not for everyone, but I can help you investigate it. You can claim this for up to eight months in your first year in the US. After one year, you are expected to be able to stand on your own two feet.

Work and stay in the US

You are a refugee. You fled from your country and had nowhere else to go. As a result, you can stay in the US – until further notice. Should conditions in your home country improve and you are no longer afraid, you can return.

With your refugee status, you can obtain a US social security card. I can help you with this.

You can also apply for an EAD. This is an 'Employment Authorization Document.' You don't have to pay for your first EAD, but you must renew it annually.

Refugees as workers

American companies are welcoming refugees. They want to give these people opportunities in their new home.

In a recent study, employers' experiences with refugees were put under the microscope. It was found that refugees are employees that stay. They are eager and grateful, with a wonderful sense of loyalty. For businesses, a higher retention rate among employees means cost savings.

The study found that refugees are very enthusiastic about starting contributing to their communities. One respondent said that the minute a refugee gets a job 'he stops being a refugee.'

Pay US taxes, and more

Even as a refugee, it is your responsibility to pay income tax. There are non-profit agencies out there that will help you. If you move, you must let the USCIS know. A male refugee must also register for 'selective' military service.

Traveling in and out of the US

You may, but not to your home country

Refugees to the US may travel. However, you must have a Refugee Travel document for when you re-enter the US. Even if you don't have a passport, this document will be accepted as a passport equivalent.

Beware though! Refugees that travel back to their home country are frowned upon. Why would you do that? You fled the country because you feared for your life. If you go back, it might be considered that you had given up on your refugee status.

How long am I allowed to stay in the US as a refugee?

The good news is, once you are allowed into the US, you can stay indefinitely. The whole idea behind being a refugee is that you can find safety in the US, and you can start building a new life. Once you are no longer afraid of being persecuted, you can return to your home country.

After one year in the US, you can also start the process of getting a permanent legal status.

Problems refugees face in the US

It is not easy for refugees to rebuild their lives. I, for one, will never forget that it can be traumatic circumstances that brought you to the US in the first place.

Many refugees come to the US with literally nothing to their name. They don't know anyone. Although the US government helps and gives assistance, the adjustment process can be laborious.

One of the problems refugees face once they come to the US is that they must find a job within the first year. This pushes them towards taking any job they can find, and not necessarily a long-term, satisfying career.

Language can be a huge problem. Yes, language classes are often provided, but a lack of transportation to classes or poor teachers can be a problem. Refugees are, therefore, not able to speak English quickly, making it harder for them to find work.

Many refugees have health problems. After living in severe conditions for long years, it might be difficult for these people to work or find work.

I pride myself on being not just a lawyer, but I am aware of these (and other) difficulties. If you make use of my services, I will do my very best to help you overcome these obstacles.

Must I go back to my country?

Most refugees return to their places of birth or their homelands when stability returns. Host countries like the US are often unable to accept refugees permanently. Resettlement permanently in the US is an option, but it is not open to everyone.

Most refugees, therefore, must voluntarily return to their home countries at some stage or another.

Voluntary return

For our booklet, I can only tell you that there is a whole policy set out of how refugees can return to their home country voluntarily. The UNHCR has a handbook for this. Should you need any information about this, I can explain it to you.

Put simply, though, if a return to your home country is deemed feasible, the UNHCR will refer you to the IOM.

'IOM' stands for the 'International Organization for Migration.' They administrate a program under which travel to your home country can be facilitated. The process of getting you home can take up to three months.

The idea is for refugees to return to their home country in an orderly and humane way. Your return and your reintegration to your home country must be planned appropriately. In the US, this is done by Assisted Voluntary Return and Reintegration (AVRR) programs where administrative, logical, and financial support might be given to refugees.

How can I stay in the US permanently?
From refugee to green card status

It is called adjustment of status

After one full year in the US, a refugee can start the process of applying for a green card. You first adjust your status to a lawful permanent resident.

The one year is calculated from the date on your I-94 form (refugee form). It is required that you do this.

Why should I apply for a green card?

It is the first step on the road to becoming a US citizen. Once you have an official green card, you'll be allowed to travel freely, become eligible for scholarships and government benefits, and more.

It is possible that your refugee status can be revoked if you no longer qualify as a refugee. It is better to start the process of applying for citizenship.

But the deadline has passed

You've been in the US for more than one year. What now? Is it impossible for you to get a green card?

The USCIS may overlook this in some cases, especially if the situation in your home country is still the same, and you've been a good citizen. I would advise you, however, not to count on this. Rules are still rules, and it is better not to take a chance if you still have some control over it.

If you missed the deadline, I would take special care of your application. We must set out clearly why this happened and assure the authorities that the situation in your home country is still unsafe for you.

Documents to apply for your green card as a refugee

The good news is that the application for a green card is free.

There are quite a few forms that must be submitted to the USCIS.

There is a form to adjust your status, a form to be filled out by your attorney if you are represented by one, and biographic information.

You must have had all the required vaccinations and perhaps a full medical exam based on your history. If you have ever been arrested or detained, you must show your criminal record.

You must have evidence of your refugee status, proof that you've lived in the US for the previous year, photos, and more.

If English is not your first language, you can include documents in your own language. However, they must be translated into English.

What happens after?

Once you've submitted your adjustment of status application, you will be notified by the USCIS once they have received your request.

Next up is a biometrics appointment. The USCIS will invite you to a meeting so that they can take your fingerprints, your photo, and your signature.

They will now check to make sure that you haven't committed any crime while you were in the US. If you have a common name, this might take a while. You might be called in for an interview if the USCIS has any questions for you about your eligibility. Usually, though, a green card application does not require an interview.

The good news is that once you get your green card, the day that you **entered** the US as a refugee will be used on your 'adjustment of status' document. You'll already have one year of permanent residence in the bank! There is, therefore, only four more years to go towards US citizenship.

How I can help you?

I can help guide you through the process. I will give you the facts about what forms you need to fill out for the USCIS, and what the basic requirements are. I'll help you to fill out the paperwork correctly, and together, we shall submit everything to the USCIS.

Other options available to you

There are other options available to you if you don't want to go through the lengthy process of becoming a refugee.

We are going to discuss this in the following pages.

In short, you can apply for Asylum status. If denied, you can still present your case to the Immigration Court. This process can be quite over-whelming, and you will need the assistance of an experienced immigration lawyer. Certain waivers also might apply to you. We will discuss that too.

Asylum status

Why seek asylum?

Every year, thousands of people come to the US because they fear for their lives. They might already have suffered harassment or torture, **or** they fear that it is going to come their way.

People seeking asylum can be persecuted because they are/were a member of a particular social group, because of their political views, race, religion, or nationality.

There is no fee to apply for asylum. If you are found eligible, you will be allowed to stay in the US. You must apply in writing within one year of arriving in the US. A spouse and children can also be included in an application. I can help you with this, as it can be tricky.

How do asylum seekers differ from refugees?

In the previous section, we've discussed refugees in detail.

In short, a refugee is **outside** of the US at first. He/she proved to the USCIS that they fear for their lives. They must receive a referral, and after being approved, they can move to the US and be resettled.

An asylum seeker is different in the sense that he/she **has arrived** in the US already. To ask for asylum is to ask for a sort of legal protection. You also must prove that you were oppressed in your home country and that it would be impossible for you to return.

Two paths to asylum

Affirmative – or defensive asylum

It is impossible to get asylum to the US without physically being **either** inside the US at the time, or at a US border. The very purpose of asylum is to protect and to ensure that these people are not thrown to the wolves.

The one path to asylum is called 'affirmative' asylum. This when a person declares to the USCIS (within one year of arriving in the US) that he or she will be applying. A USCIS officer decides their plight.

In 'defensive asylum,' a person is on the brink of being removed from the US by an immigration judge. Such a person doesn't have documents or is in violation of status but is found to have a **credible fear** of persecution.

1. Defensive asylum – applying at a US border

It might be possible for you to get into the US with a tourist visa. It can give you a little more time to find a lawyer inside the US to help you prepare your case. Make sure that you are let into the US before you ask to apply for asylum. You can mail an application to the USCIS. The best would be, however, to get an immigration attorney like me to help you.

Why should I avoid requesting asylum at a US border?

- A border inspections officer has the power to find you inadmissible and deport you. You will not be allowed to return to the US for five years. If the border official believes that you committed fraud in any way or if you don't have the correct travel documents, they can follow a quick procedure called 'summary exclusion.' The only way to convince the officer to allow you entrance is if you can make your reasons for seeking asylum very clear. It must be **compelling.**

- Another reason not to just appear at a US border is the Trump administration. Asylum seekers are deterred from entering the country. There are many ways they are doing this. We won't go into too much detail here, as the situation is changing day by day. It is enough to say that it is not that easy anymore to just be allowed into the US.

What will happen?

A USCIS asylum office will meet with you within a day or two. The officer will give you a 'credible fear' interview.

The purpose of this is to see if there is a possibility that you will win your case for asylum. Is your request really based on fear of persecution? The interview is supposed to happen within a day or two, but it has been known to take much longer.

This person will make the call if you indeed are afraid of persecution. If the person does not believe you, you can ask to be taken to immigration court. The judge will decide your fate within seven days, either in person or by telephone.

If you don't ask for the immigration court, <u>you will be deported immediately.</u> You cannot come back to the US for five years.

Should the judge find you do have a credible fear, a full hearing will be scheduled. For this, you will need an immigration attorney like me to help you state your case.

While you are waiting

While you are waiting to see a USCIS officer, you will be held at a detention facility. A type of 'parole' might be possible, but only if you can prove that you have family in the US, can post a bond, and show that someone can financially support you until a decision is made on your case.

The Trump administration – what is the situation now?

I must be honest with you. America might not be such a good haven for those fleeing persecution anymore.

Central Americans at the US-Mexico border, for example, are now almost totally blocked and can't seek asylum in the US anymore. In effect, America is saying that you must try and seek shelter elsewhere first, before turning to the US.

It is estimated that more than 40,000 Central Americans are being turned away at the border and are forced to wait in Mexico until their fate is decided. People are also sent back to their native countries without any thought given to the risks for them.

A lot of asylum-seekers enter through the southern border. They come from virtually every corner of the world: from Egypt and Iran to Zimbabwe and Nepal.

The 'remain in Mexico' policy is fraught with danger. People are beaten, raped, and even kidnapped.

Even if you make it to the front of the line, you may still also be turned away under other policies, such as you must instead seek asylum from one of the other countries that you've passed through on your way to Mexico.

More than 10,000 people were waiting at the border in September 2019. Among them, there are mothers and children. Everyone is entitled to a 'credible fear' interview, but under the asylum ban, no one really knows how these interviews are being conducted. Some people are subjected to many interviews over time, led by untrained border officials.

Of course, not everyone is happy with this.

The Supreme Court in the US said that there are decades of longstanding practices that are now being disregarded. Vulnerable people are getting hurt. Children are being taken away from their parents, Muslims are banned from the US, and Central Americans are being shut out.

The American dream is not open to everyone anymore. Donald Trump has a hardline approach to immigration, and it is not likely that this is going to change anytime soon.

We feel we must be honest with you about this.

Seeking asylum at the border, in this time and age, might not be your best route. Speak to me about other options available to you. For example, a better way would be, if it is at all possible, to seek asylum **from within** the US.

2.   Affirmative Asylum

If you can successfully enter the US, you'll have more time to apply for asylum. This is where I come in. I can help you to prepare all the necessary documents and fill in forms. Records of a personal nature are ideal. They must show that you've been arrested in the past, suffered injuries, or show the conditions of the country you are fleeing from.

There is also some 'backup' for which you can apply, such as the 'Withholding of Removal' or protection under the 'Convention Against Torture.' Ask me about it.

Eventually, you will be granted an interview at a USCIS asylum office – although you must be prepared to wait a long time, for some, up to two years. Should your case be denied, the asylum office will refer your case to the immigration court. If you are you not successful in court, you can appeal the judge's decision.

Applying for asylum is not an easy process. You must be able to put together a convincing account of what happened to you. You can spend years pursuing your application while you have no right to work in the

US legally. You must, therefore, have the financial means to support yourself while waiting.

It is best to hire an immigration attorney like me to help you from the start.

Did you know?

- You may apply for asylum regardless of your immigration status.
- You must do so within one year of your arrival in the US.

If you've been in the US for longer than one year, but you want to apply for asylum, there are some exceptions to the rule.

If you can show that your circumstances changed drastically and that you are now eligible for applying for asylum, you may still do so.

What counts for this?

- Conditions in your country changed.
- Applicable US law changed, and you are now eligible for asylum.
- You are at greater risk.
- Perhaps you were dependent on someone else's pending asylum application. If you lose that spouse or parent, you can still file an asylum application of your own even if the one-year time period has elapsed.

It can also be that the reasons why you delayed to file for asylum are very valid.

- You were persecuted or harmed. You were ill or physically disabled.
- Perhaps you've had a lawyer who took you for a ride and did

not represent you accurately. This is also a reason ('ineffective assistance of counsel') that you can offer why you are filing a 'late' application. There are some conditions that you must be aware of if you choose to go this route. I'd be happy to explain everything to you.

However, under the circumstances, you must still file your application within a reasonable time.

Can I be barred in applying for asylum from within the US?

You can. If you've previously applied and were denied, you will not be allowed to apply again, except if you can show that circumstances changed drastically.

If there is a third country that can instead take you, you can also be barred from applying in the US.

Steps to apply for affirmative asylum

- You must be physically present in the US.
- Remember the one-year rule!
- You submit a form to the USCIS (Form 1-589).
- If you are not approved, you can turn to the immigration court. (See our next section.)
- You will not wait in prison or be detained in any way while you are waiting on the outcome.

How long will the whole process take?

Usually, under normal circumstances, the process will take about six months. It will depend, however, if there are extraordinary circumstances or not.

Can I bring someone to help me with my asylum interview?

Yes. You do have the right to bring an attorney with you to your asylum interview. You can also get help from the United Nations High Commissioner for Refugees.

To represent you, an attorney must:

- Be qualified to practice law.

- Have nothing against him that will restrict him to practice law.

The attorney can be from out of state. In fact, **any** attorney may represent you before the USCIS – they just must be eligible to practice law.

And if English is a problem?

If English is not your first language and you don't speak it fluently, you can bring an interpreter to your asylum interview. The USCIS does not provide this service. You must bring your own interpreter.

Your attorney is not allowed to speak for you, nor any witness testifying on your behalf. A reputable service must also translate documents that are not in English.

Everything is done. What now?

It is possible to find out the status of your pending asylum applications.

You can write and ask, or you can visit the office with jurisdiction over your case. You can also check online if you have your receipt number.

The information you provided is protected and may not be shared with any third party.

Please speak to my office to see how I can help you.

Can I stay in the US?

Added benefit

An added benefit of a pending or approved asylum application, is of course, that you can stay, live, and work in the US.

This section looks at what happens next after you have applied for asylum following the correct procedures.

In limbo – waiting while your asylum application is pending

So, you've filled out Form I-589 and submitted all the supporting documents. You are allowed to remain the United States while the USCIS is deciding on the outcome (or even while your case is pending in immigration court.)

Perhaps the waiting time will be short. In some cases, however, it may take several years for your application to be processed.

Please note: A pending application does not mean that you have a lawful or permanent status in the US. It is not like a green card or any other form of citizenship.

However, you are NOT 'unlawfully' in America. The fact that you are 'in the system' and that your application is being processed, gives you the benefit of the doubt. As long as you don't violate any rules, you can stay in the US safely.

Intermediate Benefits

After 150 days of waiting

So, you've been waiting for more than six months, and nothing has happened. No 'approval' or 'denial' has come forth from USCIS.

The good news is that you are now eligible for work authorization. By law, immigration officials can decide on work authorization once this period has elapsed.

But, remember, the clock can be paused during the process. If **you** have caused any delays somewhere in the process of asylum (for instance if you rescheduled an appointment for an interview), the number of days will be added to the entire 150 days. The 150 days officially starts ticking after all the required documents are in, and all the preliminaries are over.

In short, therefore, an asylum applicant can apply for an EAD when he/she has accrued 150 days on her asylum clock and USCIS can grant an EAD once 180 days have accrued on the clock.

A work permit

Your work permit is called an EAD ('employment authorization document'), and it will be mailed to you. The permission allows you to work for two years. The first document is free, but if you need more, you will be charged a fee. You are entitled to apply again for an EAD while your asylum case is still pending.

With the EAD, you can do almost anything. The only positions that you will not be allowed to take would usually be in government or high-security jobs. These jobs require a green card (permanent residency status), which you don't have.

With the EAD comes a social security number

You will receive a card with your social security number that says that you can work with DHS authorization. This means that the Department of Homeland Security knows of you and your status.

A social security number is helpful in the sense that you will be able to apply for a driver's license, open a bank account, get a credit card, a cell phone, and many other things.

You're approved!

Welcome to the US

At the end of the whole process, if you were approved as an asylee, you can live and work in the US indefinitely.

Theoretically, when the situation improves in your home country, your asylum status can be terminated, although this rarely happens. After one more year, you can apply for permanent residence (a green card).

The benefit of government assistance

It is possible to get help with housing, employment, and more once your application has been approved. Act quickly, because some of these benefits are only available for a small period for new asylees.

You may also qualify for food stamps, Medicaid, or Obamacare subsidies.

I can help you with this, as some of these government assistance programs are only available in individual states and might have some tests for eligibility.

Your asylum application was denied

If your case was not approved, you most probably would be referred to the immigration court so that you can be removed from the US.

However, it is not always as clear-cut. If you are in the US under some other valid status (for example, under a student visa and you are attending classes), you will be allowed to keep your current immigration status although asylum was denied.

We will discuss the immigration court and its procedures in detail in the next section.

If, however, there is an order of removal against your name, you may not return to the US legally for the next five years. Even after that, it will be a struggle to get a visa to visit the US, as officials will be suspicious of your intentions.

There is no need to despair. With my help, we can explore all the options available to you.

From asylee to the green card holder

There is a list of requirements that you must meet to formally apply for a green card. I am not going to discuss all of it here, but the most important is that you must be physically present in the US at the time of the filing. You must have been present in the US for the past year, and you must continue to meet the criteria of an asylee.

Furthermore, you must be 'admissible' to the US. There are grounds of inadmissibility that may apply to you, but I will discuss this in full with you. Some of these grounds may be waived and a relief granted. We will discuss waivers in a separate section later on.

The list of documents needed to become an official American is quite long. I'll walk you through everything, don't worry. Just to get an idea: you'll need forms, proof of your asylum status, evidence of your one-year stay in the US, photographs, copies of passport pages, and more.

Family members of asylees can also apply for green cards. There is a separate process for them to follow.

I can help you with all of this.

◆ ◆ ◆

CHAPTER 8
IMMIGRATION COURT

What is the Immigration Court?

Independent court systems

The United States of America is a fascinating country. It has quite a few autonomous court systems. For example, the federal government has its own system. But it is not all! Every state in America operates its own court system.

But, did you know that there are also specialized courts that are equipped only to hear cases on specific topics? The Immigration Court is such a dedicated court system, and it handles only immigration cases.

An administrative court

The department of Justice in the US runs the Immigration Court as an administrative court.

In total, there are more than 55 physical immigration 'courts' in America. More than 300 Immigration judges work here.

The responsibilities of the Immigration Court

Immigration courts handle (and judge) any court case that has to do with any immigration issue. An immigration court can:

- Grant legal status to foreign nationals.

- Have people removed or deported from the US – especially if they committed an immigration violation.

- Hear appeals from foreigners seeking asylum.

How does immigration court work?

As we've mentioned above, people end up in immigration courts for a myriad of reasons. You can apply for asylum, request a 'cancellation of removal' so that you can stay in the US, or you can be in the process of becoming a permanent US citizen.

We've discussed the processes above in the previous sections. You go to immigration court if you are a refugee or asylee in America.

Overloaded

Immigration courts are often overloaded with cases. In March 2018, it was reported that immigration courts in the US were struggling with more than 340,000 active cases. They operate on a tight budget and have less administrative support than district court judges.

The system is congested. An immigration case can take several years to complete.

What is different in an immigration court?

Immigrants do not receive the same constitutional protections as other people in the US. For example, this court does not appoint a lawyer to help you.

You must appoint your own attorney, or if you're lucky, someone might represent you 'pro bono.' This means that the lawyer agrees to take on your case without expecting to be paid. Less than 40% of all immigrants have an attorney to help them.

The process begins

A notice to appear

The process that leads to the Immigration Court begins when US Immigration and Customs Enforcement (ICE) issues you a 'notice to appear.'

It is called NTA for short. This document charges you. It accuses you of being in the US without authorization. A lawyer representing Department of Homeland Security (DHS) will face you in court.

Why is the NTA important?

- It states the specific legal reasons why officials believe you are unlawfully in the US.
- It gives you notice that you will be scheduled for immigration proceedings.

Within a few days or a month (who knows?) of receiving an NTA, you will be notified where and when to appear for your first hearing in the Immigration Court.

It is essential to note the **date and time** of your hearing. If you miss it, you could be ordered to leave the US immediately.

Please note that not all people are in the immigration court due to removal proceedings. Asylum proceedings, for instance, are usually handled in a single hearing and completed quickly.

My best advice will be for me to hear your story. Why not tell it to me? I can then try to give you a more realistic timeline of what to expect from the immigration court.

Is there a method to the madness?

Let us walk you through a typical immigration court proceeding. What can you expect?

We must, however, state here that no immigration court case can be 'typical.' Each case is different and has a different set of facts. The outcome of your case will hinge on a nuance of the law unique to your case study. Yours can take months to complete.

A licensed immigration attorney will significantly help your case if you can afford one.

Three stages of Immigration Court hearings

There are three stages in an Immigration Court case. First, you get a 'master calendar hearing' or an initial hearing, then an 'individual' hearing,' and lastly, 'post-hearing proceedings' are not unheard of.

1. Fifteen minutes in a Master Calendar Hearing

Yes, this hearing can be as short as 15 minutes. The issues that are discussed, however, are not to be taken lightly. It is crucial to your case.

Use the Master Calendar Hearing to address any aspect of your case. You can, for instance, change to another court if it is more convenient for you. On a more serious note, you can also challenge your NTA and try to stop the proceedings against you.

Immigration judges can postpone or adjourn proceedings if you want to obtain legal counsel or have a pending immigrant petition that might provide relief from your removal proceedings. Depending on your reasons and available court dates, your case can be continued for a few months (or a few years.)

Should there be no issues to review, your individual hearing will be scheduled. At the end of your master calendar hearing, the court clerk will provide you with the date, time, and place.

2.   Under the microscope – your individual hearing

Does it sound daunting? It is, in a way. During an individual hearing, the court will give its full attention to you and your case. The court will then decide if you are eligible for any form of relief, and if you will be allowed to stay in the US or not.

Not 15 minutes anymore

An individual hearing can take up to four hours to complete. The court will hear testimony and review the evidence presented by you (and your lawyer.)

After all the evidence had been presented, you will be allowed to state why you should be allowed to stay in the US.

A continuance of this hearing is possible. Related issues can come up that must be resolved first, or perhaps four hours are too short to hear all your evidence. If so, your case will be rescheduled to a later date.

Once everything has been said and done, the judge will state his/her decision there and then, in open court. In rare cases, he will craft a written document. Your hearings are now finished.

3.   Post-decision appeals

All is not lost. The judge's decision can still be challenged. You can file a motion to reopen your case, or you can appeal directly to the Board of Immigration Appeals (BIA).

If you reopen the case, there are usually new facts that popped up that are now relevant to the case. This motion must be filed within 90 days after the end of your individual hearing, but exceptions are possible.

An appeal to the BIA must be filed within 30 days. The BIA reviews the decisions of immigration courts. They try to be efficient and should have an answer to your case within six months of filing.

Other long appeal processes can also be followed. I would, however, not recommend that you try to take this on, on your own. You should consider hiring an immigration lawyer, like me, to help you.

How can an immigration lawyer help you in Immigration Court?

People facing deportation or removal from the US are usually overly optimistic or overly pessimistic when it comes to the US Immigration Court.

They either think:

'I can do it! The judge will help me if I can just tell my story the right way and tug on his heartstrings. He is sure not to deport me.'

Or

'How can an attorney help me? My case is so hopeless. I'll be better off just to take my chances. It will be a waste of money to get an attorney to help me.'

Let's look at both misconceptions in turn.

You can't count on an immigration judge

There's good news, and there's bad news.

The good news is that immigration court proceedings are not as formal as ordinary US court proceedings. Everyone understands that you, as an immigrant, might not understand English that well or that you might not be as familiar with court proceedings in the US. There will be no jury – just the judge and the DHS attorney.

Also, the judge would be impartial. He or she is trained to listen to your side of the story, as well as the evidence of the DHS attorney and **consider both sides** before reaching a conclusion.

Then, there's bad news.

It is not part of the immigration judge's job description to think up legal arguments to help you. Chances are, with his very busy court docket, that the judge won't have time to probe a bit deeper and find favorable circumstances to your case that might sway his decision.

These judges have thick skin after years on the job.

'I work hard, and my family is here' might not be as a convincing argument as you might think. They've heard it thousands of times. Your reasons must be compelling and well-researched. In fact, it is tough to state your own case in immigration court. Judges deport people every day. Why would you be the exception?

Don't let this misconception rule your thinking. The judge won't help you. Only an immigration lawyer like me can. I will help you figure out a defense against deportation.

My case is so hopeless. No one can help me

That is not true. I will spend time with you to discover if the charges against you are substantiated.

We will also discuss if particular circumstances in your life can help us defend you against deportation.

Remember, US immigration laws are complex. I've spent years studying all the nuances, and I get to work with different scenarios every day. I am experienced. The possibilities open to you might not be apparent to you.

Here's what I might be able to do for you:

- I can argue that the crime you committed does not match any of the 'grounds of removability' in US immigration laws.

- I can show in some instances that you might be a US citizen after all, through parentage or a US grandparent.

- You might qualify for asylum under US immigration rules. (Please refer to our section on 'Asylum' for more information.)

- We can present a case for 'cancellation of removal.' This option makes a green card available to immigrants who have been in the US for a while, are of good character, and have close family ties here. There are also other options.

The important thing is, no matter what defense we end up choosing, I can help you make the most persuasive possible argument. After all, it is my job, and I am doing it every day. I will help you fill out the required forms, get documents together to back up everything you say, and prepare witnesses to help you in your court hearing.

Even if we lose, a solid record of information and the fact that we followed a set of procedures will make the chances you have on appeal so much stronger. At least you'll get another chance!

Your immigration hearing is your only chance to **present** your case. You'll have much better luck with an attorney at your side.

Remember, the appeal process is **not** a total review of your case. The appeals board will only decide if the immigration judge made the right decision, given the information presented. Of course, if your 'information presentation' is stellar, it can be the backbone of a successful appeals case.

Immigrants do not get free legal representation from the US government. You must hire your own lawyer if you wish for someone to represent you.

I am an immigration lawyer with my own practice. I am not 'connected' to US immigration authorities, and I am, therefore, impartial. I help clients with issues from visas, asylum, VAWA cases, to citizenship, and other matters. You can appoint me even if you live in another country.

As I said before, US immigration law is very much complicated. Hiring me might save you time, hassles, and even some money.

Seriously, you'd want to call an immigration lawyer to help you in Immigration Court if:

- You are uncertain about any immigration benefit you might be entitled to.

- You are requesting discretionary relief, such as asylum or a waiver.

- You are having trouble getting a green card, citizenship, or any other benefit.

- You need emergency immigration help.

- Removal proceedings against you have started.

When we first meet

Please bring along any personal documents that have relevance to your immigration situation. Bring your passport, any visa(s), notes from immigration court, and your marriage certificate.

Don't worry about too much, though. I will tell you what other documents might be needed that you should find or apply for.

I will ask a lot of questions in our first meeting. Most probably, I will be taking notes! It is just to help you over the long term better. I will also discuss my fee with you. It is different for each client and would depend on how complicated your case is. Please make use of the situation to tell me everything about your circumstances. Ask questions! The more I know about you, the better I will be able to help.

♦ ♦ ♦

CHAPTER 9
WAIVERS IN IMMIGRATION LAW

What is the concept of a waiver in US immigration law?

'We forgive you'

Yes, a waiver is a form of forgiveness. With it, USCIS says to particular persons:

'You have trespassed and broken one of our immigration laws. But because you explained yourself and gave us good reasons, we are willing to forgive you. You can now be admitted to the US to live and work.'

Waivers can be given to people who contracted certain diseases, who committed criminal offenses, who were 'unlawful' in the US before or had something in their past that made them 'inadmissible' before under US immigration laws.

This 'forgiveness' comes in the form of a waiver.

There are different forms of waivers and cover different circumstances.

If you request the exemption and are successful, you might receive the immigration benefit you applied for.

What does 'inadmissible' mean?

It means that the person in question is not allowed to travel to the US in any circumstances.

Let's look at a few grounds of inadmissibility under US immigration law:

Criminal grounds

If you don't adhere to standard, ethical, and honest conduct and were found guilty of any related crime, you would not be allowed into the US. Drug-related offenses, drug- or sex-trafficking, money laundering, or jail time are grounds for inadmissibility.

Health-related grounds

Dangerous physical and mental conditions, drug addiction, and transmissible diseases can bar you from entering the US.

Visa fraud

You get one chance. If you've blown it by giving false information to get a visa, you won't be allowed into the US.

Unlawful presence

Were you in America illegally before? If you entered the country as a stowaway, were smuggled in, or if you abused a student visa, it would be grounds for inadmissibility in the future.

Should you apply for an immigration waiver, your unique circumstances will be looked at. Perhaps USCIS can 'forgive' your trespasses. Your best course of action would be to speak to me. Waivers are intricate documents with lots of supportive evidence that must be attached. It is hard to do it all on your own.

A discussion of different forms of waivers

I want to start here by saying that there are quite a lot of different waivers that cover the various grounds of inadmissibility. A simple Internet search shows a bewildering range of options, different scenarios, and applications that can be hard for a non-specialist to understand.

In this section, I am going to touch on the different waivers.

Non-immigrant waivers

Form I-192

Form I-192 is an application for a specific type of waiver that allows previously inadmissible people to seek forgiveness. Should it be granted, it will enable them to enter the US on a temporary non-immigrant basis.

Who can apply?

- Someone who has no intention of staying in the US. You must be a non-immigrant.
- Someone with valid US entry documents. This means a valid US visa stamp in your passport.
- Someone seeking T- or U-visa status.
- A full Canadian citizen.

Three factors will be considered in deciding your waiver:

- The importance of you coming to the US
- The risk to society and,
- The seriousness of your previous misconduct.

How can I have a valid US visa if I was inadmissible?

Perhaps you were still admissible when you applied for your non-immigrant visa.

It can also be that you convinced US officials to give you a visa despite your inadmissibility. One example where this can happen is if you have a contagious disease. You are seeking treatment, and only doctors in the US can help you.

T- or U-visa status

We've discussed these visas before earlier in this book.

T nonimmigrant status has to do with victims of human trafficking. If you can show that you qualify for T-status, but are otherwise not admissible to the US, you can file for a waiver using the I-192. U-status is almost the same; only you must show that you were a victim of a severe crime.

Canadians

Canadians do not need US entry documents, but they can still be inadmissible. An inadmissible Canadian citizen with a valid passport must file a Form I-192 to enter the US.

Is it easy to prepare a Form I-192?

Now let's think about this for a minute. You are asking the United States of America to overlook an infringing that **actually bars** you from entering the US.

Form 1-192 is, therefore, not that easy to prepare. It should give persuasive reasons, backed up with substantial evidence so that it will convince a USCIS immigration officer to grant you a waiver.

Your evidence should explain why you were inadmissible in the first place. Say, you are ineligible because you were in jail.

You should submit a written statement explaining your situation. What happened? You should share the details of your conviction, submit official court records, and other relevant documents.

You should also explain why all this is a thing of the past and why the USCIS should allow now you to enter the US.

Let me repeat it: Your form I-192 should be compelling and convincing. I have lots of experience in compiling and submitting these forms, and I can help.

Some people have complicated cases. It might need legal research and a lot of supporting documentation that might be difficult to obtain. It would be hard to do this on your own.

You must be able to show that you have been rehabilitated, and the immigration officer must be convinced. For example, you'll have to have letters from respectable members of your community who can prove that you are of good standing. A lone statement from you is not enough. My office is experienced in preparing applications like this and in gathering the information that you might need.

Renew your waiver

Non-immigrant waivers must be renewed.

Usually, the first waiver will be valid for one year and the exemptions after that for longer – sometimes up to five years.

Remember that you must give some leeway for the application process as the processing of a waiver can take a long time.

Immigrant waivers

There are different types of waivers for immigrants, as we've discussed before.

If you are applying for a green card to the US, there are a series of different waivers connected to the various grounds of inadmissibility.

These waivers are granted once-off and are permanent, once approved.

Not all crimes can be waived. For example, USCIS sees drug crimes as very serious, and there is no immigration waiver available for this.

You must be able to prove 'extreme hardship' to a US citizen if you are to be removed from your relative or spouse. It is not enough that you and a spouse will be separated.

'Extreme hardship' comes into play, for example, if your relative is disabled and reliant on you. My office will send you for a professional evaluation by a qualified psychologist so that we will have it in writing. Extreme economic hardship can also count.

Types of immigration waivers

There are different types of immigrant waivers. Each deals with a specific set of circumstances.

The waiver helps the individual to avoid penalties and may help him/her to gain admission to the US. I must stress that every case is unique. I can help you decide what type of immigration waiver best applies to your circumstances.

You should consider getting professional help for an immigrant waiver. Your future might depend on it.

Just to recap, the grounds for inadmissibility to the US might be:

- *Health-related:* You may have a contagious disease, suffer from a dangerous disorder or addiction.

- *Of a criminal nature:* You were in prison for five years or more.

- *Misrepresentation or fraud:* You falsified information in the past.

- *Unlawful presence in the US:* You illegally came to the US.

Let's look at a few waivers that deal with these grounds of inadmissibility.

A waiver for unlawful presence in the US

This waiver is also called the Form I-601A process

So, here is the story. You entered the United States of America unlawfully ten years ago. You managed to work and live here without detection. You might even have married a US citizen.

Your spouse petitioned for an immigrant visa for you. The only way you can collect the visa is through a consulate. However, if you leave the US, you will not be allowed to enter again and be barred for ten years, since you overstayed your welcome.

(A three-year ban may also apply to your case, should you have been in the US illegally for more than 180 days, but less than one year. Without a waiver to help you, you will not be allowed to enter the US again for three years.)

The only route to go here is to apply for an unlawful presence waiver.

Apply from within the US

Since 2013, individual applicants can apply for these waivers **before** leaving the US. These applicants must be immediate relatives of US citizens (parents, spouses, or children). This was expanded in 2016 to include all eligible individuals. This new process shortens the time that family members are separated from each other.

If the waiver is approved, the eligible persons must still leave America to process their immigrant visa abroad. You cannot adjust status from within the US.

Those who are not eligible can obtain the waiver, but from outside the US. They must wait for the outcome before they can return.

Am I eligible?

You are eligible for a provisional unlawful presence waiver if:

- You are physically present in the US and older than 17.
- You are in the process of obtaining an immigrant visa.
- You can demonstrate that refusal of your admission will cause 'extreme hardship' to your American spouse or parent.

There are a few more technicalities that I will discuss with you.

Be aware, however, if you are already in removal proceedings or have a final order of removal against you, you are not eligible for this waiver.

Your approved provisional presence waiver can also be **revoked** under certain conditions, such as when the application process is ended or if the USCIS revokes the underlying approved immigrant visa petition.

As you can see, the process is full of pitfalls. Let me help you with this waiver.

The waiver is approved – what now?

When the waiver is approved, you are to leave the US to appear for your immigrant visa interview in your country. A consular officer will decide if you are eligible to receive the visa.

You must pitch for the interview, otherwise, the whole application process will be cancelled. It is possible to return to the US within one week if the proper procedure has been followed.

The Hardship Waiver or the form I-601 process

If you do not qualify for a *provisional* unlawful presence waiver, you can still file form I-601.

This is an application for an immigrant waiver on the grounds of inadmissibility. It is also called the 'Hardship Waiver.' The term 'hardship' refers to the requirement that an immigrant without the proper documents must **prove** that one of his/her relatives will suffer extreme hardship if the person is removed from the US.

Eligibility depends on the benefit you are seeking and the reason why you are inadmissible in the first place. It is complicated and can be hard to understand. I have experience in these matters and can explain the process to you.

<u>If you are inadmissible because of criminal conduct, health-related issues, visa fraud, or unlawful presence, you can apply for a waiver that addresses that specific 'problem.' Your application is Form I-601.</u>

Each of these waivers is a hardship waiver, but eligibility for each differs.

Who would qualify for this waiver?

There are two elements to consider, and you must qualify for at least one.

- You must have a family member who would suffer greatly if you are to leave the US, **or**

- You must be able to prove beyond doubt that your circumstances are unique and that you deserve a waiver.

It would be in your best interest to schedule a meeting with me so that we can discuss your case.

What relatives will qualify?

The qualifying relatives will depend on the type of waiver. For example:

- For an **unlawful presence waiver** and a **misrepresentation/ fraud waiver,** qualifying relatives are US citizens, permanent resident spouses, or parents.

- For a **criminal conviction waiver**, children are added to the above list.

How extreme is 'extreme hardship'?

It must be extreme.

You must be able to demonstrate that your qualifying relative will suffer in a way that is notably worse than just a regular family separation. Just showing financial hardship is often not enough. Emotional suffering in itself is also not 'extreme.'

It is hard for me to explain, but the fact of the matter is that your case must be entirely watertight to win your I-601 waiver case. I have years of experience in this, and I can help you.

Let's look at a few of these waivers that fall under the 'extreme hardship' waivers category.

The Criminal Conviction waiver

The US government might deem you as 'inadmissible' if you were convicted of a crime at one stage in your life. It means you won't be able to enter an immigrant visa or obtain a green card.

You may still be inadmissible, even if you were a minor at the time of the crime, or even if you never spent any time in jail for a misdemeanor.

This criminal conviction waiver 'forgives' you your trespasses.

It is important to remember that not all convictions can be 'forgiven.' The waiver is usually not for severe crimes. It would be a good idea to sit down with me so that I can give you more information about the type of offenses that can be 'forgiven.' Each case is unique, of course, and I can look at your conviction and provide you with the best assistance if I know the facts of your case.

The Misrepresentation or Fraud waiver

The definition of fraud is that you misrepresented a material fact with the intent to deceive someone. If the deciding person knew the exact circumstances, his or her decision would have been different.

USCIS sees any misrepresentation in procuring a visa, green card, or other immigrant benefits in a somber light. It may be tough to challenge a finding of inadmissibility due to fraud. I can help you sort out the details.

Perhaps:

- There was no misrepresentation.

- You made a mistake, and the fraud was not intentional or willful.

- The 'fraud' was not in connection with a material fact.

Again, to qualify for this waiver, you must show 'extreme hardship' as discussed in the previous section.

Health issue waivers

This waiver is usually granted if the applicant can show that the medical condition he or she was inadmissible for, no longer poses a risk for public health.

You can receive a waiver of a communicable disease. An immigration officer will determine if you meet eligibility requirements of the waiver, consult with others, and use his/her discretion in deciding if the waiver should be warranted.

To qualify for this waiver, the applicant must go through a list to prove his/her qualifying relationship (let me tell you about it).

The Centers for Disease Control (CDC) will look at all medical records and documents and may recommend certain conditions or controls for your situation. I have ready-made lists available so that you'll know exactly which materials we need to send in.

In the end, for this waiver, it will all depend on your documentation and the recommendation of the CDC. You don't have to prove hardship to a qualifying relative for this waiver.

At long last, the USCIS officer will use his/her discretion in granting the waiver, although it usually will be positive if the CDC does not find fault with any of your documents.

You can receive a waiver of an immigrant vaccination requirement. Perhaps you've been found inadmissible for not being vaccinated.

You may be eligible for a waiver if you've gotten the vaccination in the meantime, if it is not medically appropriate, or if a vaccination is against your religious beliefs. No qualifying relative is required here.

A panel physician will review your application.

If vaccination is against your *religious beliefs*, there are a few requirements that we have to demonstrate through documentary evidence.

- You must be opposed to all types of vaccinations in any form.
- It must be based on religious or moral beliefs.
- Your beliefs must be sincere.

A USCIS officer will use his discretion in deciding whether to grant you the waiver after reading your sworn statement.

<u>A waiver for a physical or mental disorder accompanied by harmful behavior.</u> A common condition of getting such a waiver is the applicant must see a US health care provider as soon as possible and make arrangements to receive care. A USCIS officer will determine eligibility, will consult with CDC, and use his/her discretion in granting the waiver.

No qualifying relationship is needed for this waiver. Again, a list of documents needs to be supplied to the CDC. The CDC's consultant psychiatrist will review it, and a recommendation will be provided to USCIS.

A back and forth of forms will start between USCIS, the applicant, and CDC before a waiver might be granted.

It is a long, drawn-out process, and it could be hard to keep track of what is going on. Let me help you.

The granting of the waiver is a matter of discretion in the end. For example, an endorsement of an identified US health care provider will significantly help your case.

<u>Waiver for drug abuse and addiction.</u> In general, it is tough to get a waiver for an adjustment of status for immigrants who were found inadmissible because of drugs. However, it can be overcome if you are in remission.

Immigrant waivers - Conclusion

As I said in the beginning, the different grounds of inadmissibility and the waivers available can be quite bewildering.

Please don't feel you have to figure it out all on your own. That is why I became an immigration lawyer and why I immerse myself in the law every day. I want to help. Together we will find a suitable ending for your story.

Remember, it is never over until we've exhausted all the options!

◆ ◆ ◆

CHAPTER 10
N-400: A NATURALIZED US CITIZEN

Introduction

There is another way of becoming a US citizen that we must still discuss.

If your biological (or legal adoptive) parents are US citizens by birth or were naturalized themselves before your 18th birthday, it could be that you are already a US citizen. You can then file an N-400 application to get your documents in order.

Filling in the form

Form N-400 can be submitted electronically, or can be filled in by hand, as long as you use black ink! If you don't feel comfortable answering the questions in English, we can first translate the questions for you, and you can complete a draft in your own language. We can translate everything back to English afterward.

It is not difficult to fill in an N-400 form, although I have found that some points can confuse applicants. I can clear it up for you.

General eligibility requirements to become naturalized

- You must be at least 18 years old.

- You live in the US permanently, and you've lived within your state for at least the last three months.

- You are physically in the US and have been so continuously.

- You are of good moral character.

- You support the principals and ideals of the US constitution.

- You can demonstrate a basic knowledge of US history and government and speak (and understand) basic English.

- You are willing to take the Oath of Allegiance.

Back to school

You'll see that one of the requirements is that you must be able to read, write, and speak basic English. You must also know some US history.

There are exceptions to this requirement. To sum it up shortly, if you are older than 50 years and have lived in the US between 15–20 years, USCIS will not require you to write the basic English test. However, you must still write the 'civics' test (but you can do so in the language of your choice.)

You can also be excused from the civics test due to disability or mental impairment if it has lasted for at least a year.

Biometrics appointment

After filling out the form, signing it, paying a fee, and submitting all the evidence, USCIS may ask you to appear for an interview.

They can ask you to provide fingerprints, a photo, or a signature to verify your identity. The USCIS officer might also want to ask you some additional questions or do a background or security check before deciding on your application. USCIS will inform you in writing if this is needed after they've received your application.

You can submit documents in a foreign language, but you must also provide a full English translation. The translator must sign a certification proving his/her competence and saying the translation is a true reflection of the original document.

The form itself - a hefty document

The N-400 form is divided into 18 parts. As we said, it is not challenging to fill in; one must just try to provide as much information as possible.

For example:

Part 1 deals with your eligibility to apply for naturalization. The USCIS officer will scrutinize this part to make sure that you are, in fact, eligible.

Part 2 is all about you. Your legal name, other names you've used in the past, the future name you want to use, and more.

Part 3 asks about disabilities;

Part 4 about contact information;

Part 5 about your place of residence.

Part 6 wants information about your parents, and so on.

Evidence to submit

Together with your Form N-400, you must submit:

- Photographs according to a list of specifications (I can help you with this.)

- A copy of your permanent resident card.

- A copy of your current legal marital status document.

- If you are in the military, additional documents will be required.

For your interview, there is a long list of documents to take with you. I am not going to share the list here; it will only scare you! Rest assured, however, it is relatively straightforward information that is easy to come by and to compile. I will walk you through the process, should USCIS want to schedule an interview with you.

Processing your N-400

At last! We've submitted everything. What is going to happen now?

- Your form N-400 will be rejected if it is not signed or accompanied by the correct filing fee. The form must be completed according to the specific instructions from the UCSIS.

- They will send it back to you and tell you what is wrong if they don't want to accept it in the current format. You can correct the deficiency and resubmit. Your N-400 is only considered to be correctly filed when USCIS approves it formally.

- Your form will be processed. If it is not complete, it will be rejected as USCIS sees it as if you did not establish a basis for your eligibility.

- They may ask for additional information, documentation, or evidence.

- They may request an interview.

- You will be notified of the USCIS decision in writing.

◆ ◆ ◆

CHAPTER 11
HOW TO MAKE THE BEST OF YOUR LIFE IN THE US

We've said it before. Once you get to the US, you might find that things are different from what you've imagined. Luckily, people adapt!

In this chapter, we discuss a few issues that may crop up once you are legally in the US and ready to start work.

Language barriers

It can be hard to integrate yourself into the fold of American civic life. But you are not alone! In more than 21 states in America, people who speak English 'less than very well' grew by more than 25% over the last decade.

Language access is the key to successful integration into American life.

For one aspect, without it, government services are difficult to access. Some cities are sensitive to the needs of immigrants, and they keep track of which aspects of government services immigrants need most. They then try to improve those services and try to find ways of communicating. Unfortunately, other cities are not as sensitive.

One can see why the language barrier can stretch further than just introducing yourself and trying to make friends. It impacts the very way people are starting their new life.

Typically, immigrants can learn English within 3–4 years of arriving in the US if they attend community classes regularly. However, it is not always possible if you're working two jobs to make ends meet.

What can you do?

Try your best to find out about English language classes and attend as often as possible. Even if it takes you a bit longer than the average person to learn, it will be worth your while over the long run. There are some programs where one-on-one sessions boast of great successes.

A smartphone app can help! There are lots of apps that you can download that can teach you English on your way to work or while you are cooking dinner. Practice as much as possible with neighbors and friends.

Apps can also be used to assist with communication and translate for you. You can also carry a small notebook with common phrases – where is the bathroom, how much is this item, etc. – written out for quick reference or displayed, as needed.

I'd be happy to help you find some resources if you get stuck.

Finding work

Most of the visas discussed here demand that an employer petition for you to come to the US.

Furthermore, it is illegal for you to work under a tourist or a student visa, except in certain circumstances. (Talk to me about it.)

The political climate in the United States has made the job outlook for immigrants, even legal ones, challenging.

Immigrant jobs often complement white-collar positions, but employers might force workers to work longer hours without paying overtime. They might fail to compensate employees for work done or they might not provide on the job training. Employers might fail in letting workers know about what their legal rights are.

In cases where there is provable discrimination - e.g., the immigrant has evidence from the discriminating employer in the form of a letter, email, or form – please don't hesitate to contact me.

Housing

Large cities, such as New York, typically have little in the way of affordable housing available. When an immigrant first arrives in America, their best bet for a living situation may be moving in with a friend or family member. You can also rent a room in a larger house or complex.

Rental houses and apartments typically require not only proof of an existing job through pay stubs, but often demand two months' rent up front, before ever moving in.

Additional fees, such as application fees, background check fees, and credit check fees may also apply, which is why it's essential to ensure a living situation is legitimate before paying anything.

Some unscrupulous criminals will prey on immigrants by promising a home "too good to be true" at a low price and attempting to collect payment through digital means, like a money order or an online payment processor.

Other "slumlords" may rent homes that have been illegally divided or converted into apartments that are unsafe or unsanitary, in violation of housing laws.

I'd be happy to help you. We must make sure that a landlord owns and is empowered to rent the home they have listed.

Access to services

Social programs in America can assist legal immigrants with a variety of issues, including food (EBT, or Electronic Benefits Transfer system, also called "food stamps"), healthcare, childcare, and more.

To receive these services, an immigrant must be in the country legally and able to produce paperwork to that effect.

If you are in doubt over which programs, if any, that you are entitled to, speak with me for guidance – I can point you in the right direction and ensure your paperwork is in order. If needed, we can also arrange for an interpreter to accompany you, in person or through a conference call, to help overcome any language barriers while applying.

When applying for services, always keep your identification paperwork or cards secured on your person in case they are needed. Be prepared to fill out several forms, even if the information seems redundant, as this is common when applying for services.

You should know your address, important dates (when you arrived in the country, for example), as well as information like your spouse and children's birthdays.

An immigration lawyer can usually help you bypass or work through the most challenging parts of the application process by assisting with forms and filing beforehand.

Transportation

Public transportation availability and reach varies widely depending on one's location. Certain cities in the US may only offer a limited bus system, while others may have a robust network of subways, trains, and buses.

Most public transit systems offer comprehensive websites to search for routes and timetables, and many have smartphone apps to provide real-time information on delays and route availability.

When using the transportation system, always keep your home address and destination address handy, as these will help clarify where you are going in the event of an issue that requires assistance.

Delays are common, and if public transportation is being used to get to a time-sensitive appointment, err on the side of caution, try to leave an hour or two early as a "buffer" against slowdowns, traffic, and so on.

Alternatively, provided it's affordable, you can also use rideshare services like Uber and Lyft (both available through smartphone apps) or a taxi, if one is available, to reach your destination.

Cultural differences

Americans are simultaneously intensely personable and intensely closed off, which can be dizzying for a new immigrant to navigate.

In Russia, for example, strangers may talk to one another in certain situations, but in America, it's exceptionally commonplace.

Americans tend to keep conversational topics "light" - the weather, for example, is a reasonably safe topic.

However, men should avoid making comments on a woman's appearance, particularly if they are complimenting her body – when unsolicited, this is considered harassment and can lead to issues and misunderstandings.

Avoid talking about politics or religion, as these are "hot button" issues that can rapidly lead to raised voices and tempers.

Personal space is also important: if you are close enough to read your neighbor's wristwatch, you likely need to step back a little bit, if possible.

Blunt criticisms - you have bad breath, I think you're stupid, etc. - will rarely be taken well, so be diplomatic if criticism absolutely must be offered.

Always end a request with a "please" and receive goods, services, and favors with a "thank you" and you'll be remembered as polite.

What about the kids?

Children typically assimilate better among other children than their adult counterparts.

To minimize the "leap" from native culture to an American one, proper hygiene should be observed, strongly scented colognes and perfumes should be avoided, and clothes should be clean, US-appropriate, and tidy.

This will help children of all ages make a good impression and make them approachable to new potential friends.

Parents should be prepared to help them through any cultural "growing pains," as they'll likely experience at least some culture shock when attending school.

I can help you get in touch with an English tutor before enrolment, if necessary, or arrange registration in an English as a Second Language (ESL) program at your child's school(s).

Prejudice and isolation

Unfortunately, even if an immigrant carefully learns the language and culture and takes pains to be polite, some people may act coldly or even aggressively towards them based on their country of origin.

The political climate in American right now is less-than-welcoming towards immigrants, which is why immigration lawyers are in such high demand - these professionals provide a cultural translation of sorts to help prevent vulnerable new citizens from being abused or taken advantage of.

If you are new to America, seek out other immigrants from your country, and individuals that speak your language, find a source for newspapers or entertainment programs from your country and continue to enjoy your "birth culture" as you adjust to life in America.

While becoming a resident of America can be a bit of a "learning curve," staying diligent when it comes to socializing will help prevent feelings of isolation. Even if you feel like your English is weak or worry that you won't "fit in," try it anyway – you'll be glad you did.

If you struggle with forms, rules, laws, or guidance, don't be afraid to look to me to help – that's why you connected with me in the first place.

While it will take work and patience to find your place in the United States of America, rest assured, there *is a place for you here.*

♦ ♦ ♦

CHAPTER 12
REAL LIFE QUESTIONS AND ANSWERS

In this chapter, we aim to answer your questions. In my career as an immigration lawyer, I have had to answer hundreds of questions. In this chapter, you'll find a condensed version of the most common ones. These are real issues and common problems that immigrants like you had to overcome in the past.

If you don't find an answer to **your** question here, don't despair! I'd be happy to chat and help you. Find my contact details at the end of this booklet. I can answer anything you might throw at me.

How many types of US visas are there?

There are about 200 different visas that can be used to enter the US. From tourist visas to visas for workers, students, and victims of violence. There are immigrant visas and more than 30 non-immigrant visas.

In this booklet, we aim to discuss only the most common visas that immigrants use to come to the US.

You don't have to enter the maze on your own. I can help you decide which visa will be the best suited for your unique situation.

In short, how does an immigrant become a US citizen?

Step one is to establish eligibility. You should be a permanent resident (green card holder) who has lived in the US for at least five years.

A background check and fingerprinting will follow. You will have to have an interview with the UCSIS, and your English proficiency and knowledge of American civics will be tested.

It will take about six months for your application to be approved.

What is USCIS?

USCIS stands for US Citizenship and Immigration Services. It is part of the US Department of Homeland Security and oversees legal immigration to the US.

The USCIS approves work and travel permits, green cards, and other immigration-related issues.

I am still waiting for my green card. Am I allowed to work in the US?

Yes, if you have a valid work visa (an L-1 or an H-1B, for example). If so, you can carry on working while you are applying for a green card.

How long does a green card holder have to be out of the US before he/she is considered to have abandoned their card?

If someone is out of the country for more than a year, the presumption is that the person has abandoned residence.

I got married to a US citizen. How long after my marriage can I apply for a green card?

Your US citizen husband or wife petitions for your green card by filling in forms. You will be called in for an interview after a few months.

If the interview goes well, you'll be approved for lawful conditional resident status. After being married two years, you can ask for the conditions to be lifted and you can get a green card.

What documents do I need to apply for a marriage green card?

You must prove that the sponsoring spouse is a US citizen. You must provide a marriage certificate and some evidence that the marriage is authentic. Your spouse's financial situation must also show that he/she can support you.

My father (a US citizen) died before he could sponsor me. I already was a legal resident. Can I still get my American citizenship?

I must have more information. Are you already eighteen? Did your father start the petitioning process before he died? Can you provide proof that your dad became a citizen? Have you left the US at any time and if so, for how long?

You can seek citizenship by derivation or by naturalization. I am a competent and experienced immigration lawyer who can help you. Your situation is complicated. Contact me so that we can unravel it.

How long does the H-1B process take? I need to start working soon.

The complete process to receive an H-1B non-immigrant visa can take between 4–9 months.

I was offered a job and applied for an H-1B visa but did not receive

approval yet. Is there any way that I can come to the US and start the job I was offered?

Unfortunately, not. The only way you can work in the US is if you have the correct visa that allows you to work there. USCIS will return your application to the employer who petitioned for you. Contact him/her to find out if you got approved or not.

I am in the process of switching employers on an H-1B visa. If I get denied, is it possible to find a third employer without leaving the US?

It depends. If you can do this while you still have a valid H-1B visa, it is possible. However, if you are 'out of status' at any time (therefore, without a valid work visa), it won't be possible.

I am eligible for US citizenship in about six months. I want to sponsor my unmarried son to come to the US. Should I wait until I am a citizen, or will it make no difference?

You can start the process immediately. Your petition can be upgraded as soon as you become a US citizen. If your son is not yet 21, he will qualify as a child of a permanent resident. Once you become a citizen, your son will be considered an immediate relative, and he can apply for an immigrant visa. Speak to me to help you with the different options available.

I entered the US illegally. Now, someone wants to sponsor me to work legally. Can it work?

No, you won't be able to get a green card. You'd have no status to 'adjust,' therefore you won't be eligible to get a green card.

My English is not good at all; how will I cope in the US?

Agreed, it can be quite hard to learn a new language, and it becomes more complicated with age. It also takes time and effort.

Unfortunately, you'd have to try and learn English to make the best of your life in the US. Most successful immigrants go to English classes several nights a week – even after a hard day's work. It can be done.

My husband refuses to petition me for US citizenship. We have been married for a long time and had two children who were born here. He has threatened me and won't allow me to leave the house at times. I don't want to be separated from my children! How can I stay in the US?

You are a victim of spousal abuse. The VAWA (Violence against Women Act) allows you to apply for a green card without the permission of your husband. He does not have to petition for you.

It is the whole point to the process and the act: that you don't have to be dependent on an abuser to stay in the United States. Please contact me to find out more about filing a petition under the VAWA.

My child was born in the US. Can I stay?

No, unfortunately, not if your child is still underage. Of course, your child is a US citizen upon birth if born here. However, such a child can only petition for you when he/she turns 21. There is no automatic immigration benefit for such a child's parents.

I find paperwork hard. My English is not good. How can I apply for the American visas?

Your question is the whole point of why I've written this booklet. I want to help. I am an immigrant myself, and I went through the same processes and issues that you did.

I am meticulous and experienced. First, I would meet with you to hear your life story. There are such a lot of visa options available – it is just a matter of deciding which one applies to you and your situation.

After we've decided which route we are going to take, I'll walk with you – every step of the way. It is my opinion that this is the only way of successfully immigrating to the US: if you have a professional to help you and make you aware of possible pitfalls.

It may be hard, but we'll get there in the end!

Please contact me at 212-791-7500 as soon as possible if you are considering immigration to the US.

With my social work, psychology, and legal background, I am the best person to get you and your family into the United States.

CONCLUSION

I hope I was able to answer one or two of your questions. However, I am sure you would agree, it is impossible to answer every question! You might have more.

Please contact me. I would love to help you.

My offices are located at:

225 Broadway, Suite 630

New York, New York 10007 (Manhattan)

1815 Avenue U, Suite 2

Brooklyn, New York 11229

My email address is levannyc@yahoo.com

You can also call me at 212-791-7500.

Let's start your journey together!

ONLINE RESOURCES

Immigration Law in the United States is complex and constantly changing.
Please do not attempt to navigate the immigration and visa process alone.
As you can see below, there are numerous avenues for support to immigrants.
However, only immigration law specialists like myself have the training and
experience to effectively and efficiently navigate them on your behalf.

For specific legal guidance, direction, and support, please contact my office.
I have the legal credentials, expertise, experience, and networks to support you
on your immigration journey to the United States of America.

—US Government—

**Benefits.gov – Refugee and Entrant Assistance – State
Administered Programs**

Focus: Range of government assistance programs, including support for needy
immigrants and refugees

www.benefits.gov/categories/Immigration%20and%20Refugee%20Assistance

Healthcare.gov

Focus: Health coverage for lawfully present immigrants

https://www.healthcare.gov/immigrants/lawfully-present-immigrants/

Immigration and Customs Enforcement (ICE)

Focus: Review of documentation (including visas) at US ports of entry

www.ice.gov

National Domestic Abuse Hotline – 1-800-799-SAFE (7233)

Focus: Free 24/7/365 multilingual support for any person in the United States who is experiencing domestic violence, seeking resources or information, or questioning unhealthy aspects of their relationship. A live chat is available 24/7 on the web site

www.thehotline.org/help/

National Visa Center (NVC)

Focus: Central pre-processing of all classes of approved visas

travel.state.gov/content/travel/en/us-visas/immigrate/national-visa-center.html

Social Security Administration (SSA)

Focus: Supplemental Security Income (SSI) for Non-Citizens (Sept. 2019)

www.ssa.gov/pubs/EN-05-11051.pdf

Student and Exchange Visitor Program (SEVP)

Focus: International academic and vocational students and exchange visitors

www.ice.gov/sevis

US Citizenship and Immigration Services (USCIS) – Citizenship Resource Center

Focus: Educational tools and resources for preparing for US citizenship, including resources in up to seven languages

https://www.uscis.gov/citizenship

US Department of Education

Focus: Educational resources for immigrants, refugees, asylees, and other new Americans, including multilingual language assistance

www2.ed.gov/about/overview/focus/immigration-resources.html

US Department of Health and Human Services – Office on Women's Health

Focus: Violence against immigrant and refugee women

www.womenshealth.gov/relationships-and-safety/other-types/immigrant-and-refugee-women

US Department of Housing and Urban Development (HUD) – Office of Fair Housing and Equal Opportunity (FHEO)

Focus: Enforcement of US government laws concerning non-discrimination in housing

www.hud.gov/program_offices/fair_housing_equal_opp/fair_housing_rights_and_obligations

US Department of Justice – Office for Victims of Crime

Focus: Information, resources, and contacts in support of justice and healing for victims of crime

www.ovc.gov/help/index.html

US Department of Labor

Focus: Workplace rights

www.dol.gov/general/topics

US Department of Labor – Employment & Training Administration

Focus: Permanent labor certification by employers (not employees)

https://www.foreignlaborcert.doleta.gov/perm.cfm

US Department of Labor – Occupational Health and Safety Administration (OHSA)

Focus: Preventing and investigating retaliation against employees (including immigrants) for reporting occupational health and safety issues in the workplace

www.whistleblowers.gov/

US Refugee Admissions Program (USRAP)

Focus: Assessing cases referred by organizations such as the UNHCR

www.uscis.gov/humanitarian/refugees-and-asylum/refugees/refugee-eligibility-determination

Websites of US Embassies, Consulates, and Diplomatic Missions

Focus: Starting point for visa applications from abroad. Find the one nearest you where you will apply and be interviewed

www.usembassy.gov/

—Non-Profit Organizations—

American Immigration Council (AIC)

Focus: Among its mandates, the AIC sponsors interns and trainees under the Exchange Visitors program

https://exchange.americanimmigrationcouncil.org/

Business Center for New Americans (BCNA)

Focus: Business loans, home ownership, and savings

https://nybcna.org/

International Student – International Communications

Focus: Choosing the optimal communications for staying in touch with your home country while abroad

https://www.internationalstudent.com/international-communications/

International Student – Study in the USA

Focus: Wide range of information resources for students hoping to study in the US

https://www.internationalstudent.com/study_usa/

United Nations High Commissioner for Refugees (UNHCR)

Focus: International coordinating agency for protection of refugees, asylum-seekers, and stateless people and how to get help

https://help.unhcr.org

Made in the USA
Coppell, TX
30 January 2024

28404119R00085